HIGHWAYS AND BYWAYS OF CALIFORNIA

HIGHWAYS AND BYWAYS OF CALIFORNIA

by CLIFTON JOHNSON

Illustrations by Tom Whitworth

Whitworth & I • Santa Fe, New Mexico

Whitworth and I edition, March 2026

The enclosed excerpts — "On the Borders of Mexico", "A Rustic Village", "Spring in Southern California", "Santa Barbara and its Historic Mission", "A Vale of Plenty", "April in the Yosemite", "Around the Golden Gate" and "Among the Shasta Foothills" — originally appeared in *Highways and Byways of The Pacific Coast*, first published by The MacMillan Company in 1908 as part of the *Highways and Byways of America* series. This is an abridged republication from the 1915 printing, which was titled *Highways and Byways of California*, with minor editing of the original text and new illustrations. A few short racially offensive passages have been omitted.

Whitworth and I - Press

Whitworth and I, LLC
223 N. Guadalupe Street, Box 283
Santa Fe, New Mexico 87501

www.whitworthandi.com

Library of Congress Control Number: 2026932738

ISBN: 978-0-9771655-1-3

CONTENTS

Introductory Note

The several volumes in this series have as a rule very little to say of the large towns. Country life is their chief topic, especially the typical and the picturesque. To the traveler, no life is more interesting, and yet there is none with which it is so difficult to get into close and unconventional contact. Ordinarily, we catch only casual glimpses. For this reason, I have wandered much on rural byways and lodged most of the time at village hotels or in rustic homes. My trips have taken me to many characteristic and famous regions; but always in both text and pictures I have tried to show actual life and nature and to convey some of the pleasure I experienced in my intimate acquaintance with the people.

These "Highways and Byways" volumes are often consulted by persons who are planning pleasure tours. To make the books more helpful for this purpose each chapter has a note appended containing suggestions for intending travelers. With the aid of these notes, I think the reader can readily decide what regions are likely to prove particularly worth visiting, and will know how to see such regions with the most comfort and facility.

Clifton Johnson
Hadley, Mass.

ON THE BORDERS OF MEXICO

What I saw of Arizona and Eastern California as I sped across them on the journey to the coast was for the most part barren, parched and forlorn to the last degree. As one of my fellow tourists remarked, "I don't see what all this land is good for except to hold the world together."

But suddenly the desert was left behind and we were amid blossoming gardens and green, luscious fields, and orange orchards with their dark, vigorous foliage all a-twinkle with golden globes. What a land of enchantment it did seem after those long days on the train hastening over the frosty and arid plains, and how the fresh full-leaved greenery did delight one's heart! All things were growing and flourishing, the weeds were getting rank, the wildflowers were in bloom, and everywhere in home yards were callas and other hot-house and summer flowers in prodigal profusion.

To get as near the tropics on our west coast as possible I journeyed to San Diego, and on the way thither I had my first sight of the Pacific rolling its

thunderous surf up on the beach and dimpling softly under the half clouded sky as far as the eye could reach. At San Diego, I renewed my acquaintance with it, and spent much of the first day rambling along the waterside. I lingered longest in the section where the fishermen dwell. Their little cottages are many of them on piles and are over the water at high tide. This has its advantages, but there had been a storm the previous Sunday which made the pile-dwellers wish their homes were on the firm ground. It was as wild a gale as even the oldest inhabitant could remember, and the wind rose till the spray flew over the cottage platforms and wet the floors inside. To make matters worse the little rowboats and the fishing craft and some heavy timbers got away from their moorings in the harbor and butted into the supporting piles of the dwellings.

"Oh, yes," said one lady, "it blowed so hard it done quite a good deal of damage. You see our garden out in front here. Everythin' in it was gettin' to look real nice; and now notice that yaller blossoming willow bush. It was crowded full o' flowers, but the storm just nacherly pretty near broke it down."

"We was lucky," said her husband, "that we didn't get into no badder troubles. Some houses was let down into the water and knocked all to pieces. Our house come near goin'. It had only two piles left under the middle; and it got twisted so the door wouldn't open, while we was still inside. We begun to think we'd be drown, and I took a hatchet and pried off a window-casing. I'd 'a' knock the whole darn lights out rather than stay in there any longer. When we escaped I tried to save some boats that jammed in here next us. But when I had one partly pulled out a big wave piled twenty or thirty more on top, and I give up. After the storm I saved some broken pieces so I got a little of my damage back. I have sold part of them and they will furnish me tobacco money to last a while, anyway.
"I'm thinkin' it's goin' to rain again," he remarked as we were about to part. "I have a crooked toe that was shot in the Civil War, and that pains me every time the weather's turnin' bad. It never ain't failed me yet, and I

feel a storm is comin' now."

I was still wandering about exploring the town when I was accosted by a bareheaded, swarthy gypsy woman who wanted to tell my fortune. The charge was two bits, she said, and I produced the money. Then she made a poor pretense of glancing at the lines of my hand and mumbled a sing-song repetition with slight variations about my having had much trouble, asserting in conclusion that, "You have make considerable money, but you spend it easy."

She hit it right about the spending so far as the quarter I had just parted with was concerned. Next she pulled a couple of little threads out of the fringe of her shawl, and had me tie two knots in one of them and repeat after her, "Go way trouble." "Go way my bad luck."

That done she crumpled up the knotted string, slyly substituted the other, which she had kept concealed, and told me to pull it out—when lo! the knots were gone. Lastly she gave this thread a twist about one of my buttons and affirmed that if I didn't "tell nobody about it for eight days" I probably wouldn't have "no more trouble and bad luck." To make the thing certain, however, she wanted another quarter.

San Diego appealed to me most forcibly in the suggestions one caught everywhere that the place never experienced our savage Eastern winter. Yet there were chilly mornings and days of wind or rain, when a fire was a comfort. Otherwise everything conspired to make one feel it was early summer instead of March.

One morning I visited Old Town, an outlying suburb, which in the early days constituted all there was of San Diego. At that time the site of the present city was a sheep pasture. The parent village is pretty dead now, and many of the ancient adobe structures are in ruins, but others are still intact and occupied. Such structures are particularly interesting, because their massiveness gives them an air of repose and permanence, and because they are characteristic of the common method

of building in the days when California was a part of Mexico. The material employed is a very sticky, dark brown clay fashioned into blocks about four times the size of an ordinary brick. Sometimes straw cut up into pieces an inch or two long was worked into the clay mud. Wet clay was used as mortar when the blocks were laid. The timbers of the floors, doorways and windows were built in as the walls were in process of erection.

Eight miles from Old Town, up a neighboring valley, is the remains of an ancient Spanish Mission which I decided to see. The valley is wide, and its basin is mostly cultivated. Much of it was growing to barley, oats and other grains, then knee high, and there was Indian corn well started, and melons just coming up, and an abundance of garden truck of all sorts ready for market. The finest tract was farmed by a Chinaman. He had many acres as level as a floor and his crops were thriving admirably, but his home buildings were dilapidated, and even the house a mere shack. The litter of work and carelessness was dubiously evident all about, and the premises were so odorous that it was no joke to get to leeward of them.

Judging from the Chinaman's success, I imagined he would have rather a rosy opinion of the region, but some of the other dwellers in the valley were decidedly pessimistic. "California is overrated," said one of them to me. "Every farm in the state is for sale. You need money to enjoy this country, and it takes a good big purseful to run a farm and get it into shape to be profitable. A poor man, or a man of moderate means has no chance. He travels uphill all the time and often in the end has to sell out for a song. Lots of people have an idea there's money in fruit, but I've noticed our fruit growers usually make a profit one season and lose the next nine."

The man did not appear very energetic, and his land did not look as if he worked it with much vigor or judgment. No doubt he painted the country in tints out of his own experience. Another man I talked with was a grizzled old fellow of a different type. He was carrying a post on his shoulder, and when I the accosted him he dropped the butt end to the ground. Every few minutes he shifted the post up to his shoulder as if about to go on, but the conversation would take a fresh start and down would go the post once more. He did not agree with the neighbor whom I have quoted. "Oh, no," said he, "not every place is for sale. The majority are, but there's exceptions. I wouldn't sell mine—leastways, not unless I got a good big price for it.

"I was over in Arizona lately," he continued, "and on the train that brought me back, I had a talk with a Missouri man who was comin' to the coast to settle with his whole family, and he said, 'My little girl has been thinkin' they have gold houses out in California and gold sidewalks and gold everything. She says she reckons they have gold taters to eat.'

"It's a good deal the same with the older folks. They are often disappointed simply because they have un-reasonable expectations. Yes, that's just it, and they've got a lot to learn. It ain't no soft job here. There's plenty to do all the time, and if you want to succeed you haven't hardly got time to talk to anyone. Even an industrious man don't find it all straight sailin'. This region is naturally kind of a desert. Just now for a few years we're havin' rain, and everythin' is green and flourishin'. You couldn't have better pasturage, and we don't have to feed our stock anything in addition to what they pick up themselves, the year through. But before this wet spell there was eleven years we only had one good rain. The streams went dry, the wells went dry, and the feed all shrivelled up in the pastures. Why, we had to give stock cactus to eat. We'd make a quick brush fire and take the cactus and singe off the thorns, and that singed cactus was what the cattle lived on. I sold most of my cows at ten dollars apiece the feed got so scanty.

"Another thing we've found out is that we can't raise fruit in this neighborhood. The trees will do well for three or four years, but see here," and with his post he thumped some clay laid bare in a washed-out gully, "under the surface soil a foot or two is this old adobe, and it's got alkali in it. That's the boy that ruins the fruit trees. The roots, as soon as they strike it, crumple up, and your trees begin to croak and don't flourish any more.

"But the situation is like this—a man who comes here and works hard and uses some common sense and adapts himself to the country will prosper. One day I was callin' on a genoowine old Dutchman who is livin' a few miles away. 'Vell,' he says, 'dis desert does look fine when it rains.'

"He's got about sixteen children, and you might think he'd have trouble supportin' 'em. I mentioned something of the sort, but he replied, 'I make a living here,' and he gave a big wink and then said, 'and I makit one dollar besides.'

"So can other people."

It was a half-clouded morning, and the weather was reminiscent of a sultry day in June at home. The heat was full of moist, growing power, and the pastures and waysides were besprinkled with blossoms of every hue. Poppies, thistles and morning-glories were easily recognized, but most of the blossoms were unfamiliar, and they made a pageant of color such as the East never witnesses. One's ears were greeted with the buzz of flies, the chirrup of insects, and by the croaking of frogs on the sodden lowlands. The walk was quite delightful, though not wholly so, for some little gnats darted about my face very persistently. The road I followed was not a public way, and it was frequently interrupted by gates that I had to climb over or open, and its markings became less and less distinct till I lost them altogether. I was then in a cultivated patch of olive trees, and many of the trees were loaded with fruit, both green and ripe. The ripe olives looked very like plums, and their appearance was so inviting I tried one, but it came out of my mouth much quicker than it went in.

I wandered across several fields till I found my road again, and at last I reached the old Mission on a terrace of a steep hillslope. Much of the original buildings is gone. They were used as a cavalry barracks in the war of 1846 and later as a sheep fold, and such use, added to neglect, has left only remnants, but enough still existed of the stout adobe walls to be impressive. It overlooked the peaceful, fertile valley. Nearby, at the foot of the slope, was a grove of ancient olives musical with great numbers of birds, and on the borders of the grove was a fragment of cactus hedge and a few date palms, all that remains of the friars' garden.

This is the oldest of the California Missions.

It was founded in 1769, but the ruins do not date back to its beginnings for, in its sixth year, the Mission was attacked by hostile Indians, one of the padres was killed and the buildings burned to the ground.

By the end of the century there were seventeen more Missions, and three others followed later. It was their purpose to instruct and civilize the Indians. The founding of a Mission was very simple. After a suitable place had been selected in a fertile valley, a cross was set up, a booth of branches built, and the ground and the booth were consecrated by holy water and christened in the name of a saint. If there were Indians in the vicinity they were attracted to the spot by the ringing of bells swung on the limbs of trees, and presents of food, cloth and trinkets were given them to win their confidence. Each new Mission had at first only two monks. The booth and cross were in their charge, and they were to convert and teach all the Indians of the neighborhood. Several soldiers and perhaps a few partly Christianized Indians served as a guard and helpers. The community would have a number of head of cattle and some tools and seeds, and with this humble equipment those in charge were expected to conquer the wilderness and its savage inhabitants.

Indians were taught to cultivate the earth and to do a variety of mechanical work. They felled timber, transported it to the Mission sites, and used it, together with adobe and tiles, in erecting the churches and other buildings. Thus in time rose the pillars, arched corridors and domes of the stately structures that are still impressive even in their ruins. Gradually a village grew about each church, for the Indians were encouraged to live nearby, and some of the Mission communities numbered thousands.

The chief structure at a Mission was usually in the shape of a hollow square with a front of four or five hundred feet along which extended a gallery. The church formed one of the wings, and in the interior was a court adorned with trees and a fountain. Round about was a corridor whence doors opened into the friars' sleeping apartments, workshops, storehouses, school-rooms, etc. At sunrise, a bell was rung and the Indians assembled in the chapel for prayers. Afterward they had breakfast and were distributed to their work. At eleven they ate dinner, and work was resumed at two. An hour before sunset the Angelus bell was tolled and labor was abandoned for religious exercises in the chapel. Supper followed, and then the Indians were free to take part in a dance or other mild amusements.

The rule of the friars was in the main just and kindly. Drunkenness was punished by flogging, and the offenders in quarrels between husbands and wives were chained together by the legs till they promised to keep the peace. Fresh recruits were secured by sending out parties of Indians already attached to the new mode of life and letting them set forth to the savages its advantages, though it is said they were also sometimes captured by main force. The domestic animals imported for the use of the Missions multiplied with great rapidity, and in the care of them the Indians became very dexterous. Hides, tallow, grain, wine and oil were sold to ships visiting the coast, and from the proceeds the friars supplied the Indians with clothing, tobacco and such other things as appealed to the taste or fancy of the converts. Surplus profits were employed in embellishing the churches.

The Missions were established at about a day's journey apart on the natural route of travel along the coast, and they were the usual stopping-places for travelers. Whenever one of these sojourners arrived he was welcomed with the hospitality of the Bible patriarchs. First of all, his horse was led away to the stables, and the man was escorted to a bath. Afterward he was given a plentiful meal and a comfortable bed, and he was at liberty to stay as long as he chose.

The maximum of Mission prosperity was attained in the first quarter of the nineteenth century. The friars and their neophytes owned countless herds of cattle, horses, sheep, goats and swine, and produced from the ground all their simple needs required. At each Mission were enclosed gardens and orchards where grew a considerable variety of vegetables and many fruits, including figs, oranges, olives and grapes. But white settlers were increasing, and contact with them tended to corrupt the Indians and to make them less easily controlled. The greed of the newcomers was aroused by the wealth of the Missions in land and herds, and in 1833 they influenced the Mexican congress to pass a law secularizing the Missions and turning over their property to public purposes, except for some small allowances reserved to maintain the churches. This enabled the politicians of the period to plunder the Missions very thoroughly, and the administrators who were appointed wasted no time in getting the tangible property into the hands of themselves and their friends.

So serious was the desolation wrought, and

so evil were the effects on the Indians, that the law was rescinded, but the mischief had been done, and the Missions were not able to recuperate. The ruin was completed by the American conquest, and the few remaining Indians were driven or enticed away. That they and their ancestors had been cultivating the lands for three-quarters of a century made no difference. The Americans wishing to preempt claims did not regard the presence of Indian families or communities as any more a deterrent than they would have so many coyotes. What cared the rude frontiersmen for missionary friars or civilized Indians? They came to squat on public lands, and they not only took such tracts as pleased their fancy, but in some cases the Mission structures were demolished for the sake of the timber, tiles and other building materials that were in them.

Every visitor at San Diego makes a trip to the village of Tia Juana, just across the line in Mexico. The idea is cultivated that by doing so one will get a brand new impression and that he will see a bit of Mexico which will serve as a fair sample of the whole. It is sixteen miles down to the line, and a train takes you that far. Close by the terminus is a boundary monument, and some people find pleasure in standing with one foot in their own country and one in foreign territory. Often they have themselves photographed in that position. But the person who wants to make all he can out of the situation jumps back and forth across the line until he is tired. Then, when he reaches home and is asked if he has been to Mexico, he can truthfully respond, "Oh, yes, many times."

After you have had a look at the monument and

indulged in such extras as seem desirable, you get into an omnibus drawn by four horses, and away you go over a road that I should judge had never received any attention since it was first travelled. There are holes and ruts and bumps and sloughs unnumbered, and whenever I thought we were going to capsize in one direction, the vehicle was sure to lurch and up went the other side to the danger point. Much of the way was across a gullied, brushy level where the floods had rampaged. Worse still, we had to ford a swift and muddy river. Into it we splashed, and the horses half disappeared, while the water swashed up over the wheel hubs and barely missed coming into the 'bus.

At last we reached Tia Juana. Its attractions were not very pronounced. There was just a wide street with a few shops and saloons on either side, and at some distance a straggling of shanty dwellings. It was on a bare plateau, but along the slope that dipped to the valley grew a few groups of trees. The plain swept away to a series of mountain ridges clothed with cacti and sagebrush. Such village men as were not employed in the shops seemed to be a lot of loafers, not given to exerting themselves much beyond the smoking of cigarettes.

The one notable institution of the place is a bull-ring, and the amphitheater of seats rises conspicuously just outside the hamlet. It is the patronage of the Americans that keeps the thing going, and any Sunday on which there is to be a fight they come from San Diego in swarms. Extra trains are put on, and teams drive from the town and from the ranches for miles around to serve as stages for conveying the excitement seekers from the station to the bullring. The chief financier of the enterprise is a Mexican who has a diminutive butcher shop in the village. It seems a somewhat appropriate branch of his everyday industry, but what can one say for the Americans who encourage the savage and degrading exhibitions?

The cost is a dollar for a seat in the sun, two dollars for a seat in the shade, and the audience is sure to number at least a thousand, and may rise to twenty-five hundred. It was said that the patronage had fallen off decidedly the year before because several horses had been gored to death. This was too much for the

tender sensibilities of the American audience. The on-lookers were willing to see bulls killed, but not horses, and many of them refrained afterward from going. So now the toreadors have to fight on foot.

Between Tia Juana and San Diego is some very fine lemon country, and on my way back I had a talk with the owner of a twenty-acre orchard. "I come from Nebraska two years ago," he said, "and I wouldn't go back to live if you'd give me the whole state. It's too cold, and they have blizzards there that blow the trains off the railroad tracks. I looked around down here and found a feller that was sick of the lemon business, and we made a swap. I give him sixteen hundred acres I had in Nebraska, and he give me his twenty-acre lemon orchard. Some of my neighbors up where I come from told me I was makin' a poor bargain, but the Nebraska land was only worth about fifty cents an acre, so the value of my sixteen hundred acres didn't count up very heavy. The feller I sold to didn't really want the property, and he made another dicker and let it go for the furnishings of a shooting-gallery in Los Angeles worth very little over three hundred dollars.

"They'd been havin' a spell of dry years, and the lemon orchards wa'n't payin' expenses, but the weather turned about and the trees began to do first-rate. It beats all how they will bear. There's blossoms and green fruit of every size and the ripe lemons right on the same tree the year through. I shall clear six or seven thousand dollars this year. Of course, there's considerable expense, and I keep from two to six men at work and pay 'em a dollar and a half for a nine-hour day. I don't hire any Mexicans—I don't like their color—and I don't hire negroes or Chinamen. I do considerable myself, but I feel that I'm kind o' gettin' lazy like everybody else that lives in this climate. It's very different from what I been used to. You notice the old men here. They ain't got the vim and spirit they have in the East. Back in Nebraska, an old man would think nothing of chasing a critter that had broke loose, but take a man of the same age in California, and you couldn't get up a run with a pitchfork.

"There's something about the air that slows you down, and I have an idee that once you get used to it, you ain't really contented anywhere else. Some people recollect their old home, in New England may be, and they think they'd like to go back there to live. One man whose home was near my lemon ranch was always talkin' that way, and finally he sold out and went, but inside of two months he was back. Things there wa'n't quite like what he remembered them, and the folks he used to know was mostly gone or changed. So he decided California was the place for him."

Nearly a score of miles east of San Diego is the broad fertile valley of El Cajon. It lies among the hills with lofty rugged mountains overlooking it from farther inland, and I went to see it, attracted by the fact that it is famous for its great vineyards whence are shipped each season hundreds of carloads of raisins. An irrigating flume circles the hillslopes, but this artificial watering does not entirely take the place of rain, and in dry years the crop is sure to be a partial failure. Most of the ranches of this handsome vale were mortgaged, I was told. There are so many chances in weather, in disease, in pests, and in price that a permanent success in fruit growing in Southern California seems to be somewhat rare. It is a not uncommon belief that dry and wet periods alternate, each covering a series of several years. Things boom in the wet cycle, while in the lean years many orchards and vineyards fare so badly that they become almost worthless.

I had come to El Cajon by train with the intention of walking back, and presently I was plodding along toward San Diego, most of the time on the level mesas but now and then dipping into a valley. There were frequent orchards of oranges, grape-fruit, lemons and olives, some thrifty, some far otherwise. The orange trees, though still loaded with fruit were coming into blossom, and in places the air was honeyed with the perfume. Most of the homes I passed were common-place little cottages, frequently only a story high, apt to be ugly from plainness, but sometimes

equally ugly from over-ornamentation. Yet there were a number of really substantial and attractive dwellings, fine in themselves and charming in their flowery environment. One home had a great rank hedgerow of roses full of white blossoms, but much of the land was as wild as it ever had been and was brushed over with chaparral and other shrubs waist high. A good deal of this was government land that could be bought for a dollar an acre. The country was at its greenest, but when the spring rains were past the ground would gradually parch and by July all the fields and pastures and waysides where there was not an artificial water system would be clothed in somber brown, and they would so continue till near the end of the year.

Halfway in my journey I was overtaken by a young fellow in a buggy, and he invited me to ride. I was glad of the opportunity for I was getting weary and the landscape did not present much variety. He was from the East a twelve-month before and had been spending most of his time "cow-punching" in the mountains. He expressed the opinion that the country

offered excellent chances to make money. But, if it was easy to make, it was also uncommonly easy to spend; "and yet," said he, "you can live here as cheaply as anywhere if you choose to do so. Now San Diego is quite a resort of old Civil war pensioners. They're there on the plaza every day sitting around under the shadow of the palms. I've talked with 'em and they say a man can bach' it—that is, get feed for himself livin' as a bachelor—for a dollar and a quarter a week, and a room will cost a dollar more. So a moderate pension will support a man without his doing anything."

In my own experience, I found the gentle conditions of life were best exemplified by a man who dwelt near the beach. I had the feeling at first that I had fallen in with a shipwrecked mariner on a desert island. Just back out of reach of the waves he had a shanty seven feet one way by eight the other, and barely high enough to stand up in. It was built of all sorts of rubbish, and nearly everything in the house and round about might have been saved from some castaway vessel, and indeed was largely the salvage of the sea. The interior walls were crowded with shelves, and from frequent nails were suspended many articles of use and ornament. The furnishings included a number of pictures and newspapers and a few books. There was a bed with a coverlet made of an old sail, a chair tinkered out of some pieces of board, a rusty little stove, a muzzle-loading musket, and quantities of odds and ends. The two tiny, single-paned windows each had a board shutter inside and reminded me of the port holes of a ship.

I saw all these details with some thoroughness because I was caught by a shower and was invited to take shelter in the hermit's hut. Outside he had a shed with a roof made of an old boat turned keel upward, and he had various whirligig contrivances set up in his yard—weather vanes in the form of ships with sails set and propellers revolving, and a kind of windmill of odd construction that turned a coffee grinder.

The proprietor of this peculiar conglomerate was a Maine man originally and was a person of intelligence and some education. His chief companions were cats, and I saw half a dozen or more dozing around the premises. He got all the wood he needed to burn from the sea, and the sea furnished him with much of his food. Most of his fishing he did with a hook and line, but sometimes used a spear when he went after halibut. His gun had been neglected of late, because the last time he fired it he was out on the water after ducks and it nearly kicked him out of his boat. The money he needed to supply his few wants he got by digging and marketing a few clams, and by taking care of some boats belonging to the town boys, and by catching crawfish which he sold for bait. During the twenty years he had lived there he had never had an overcoat. It wasn't his habit to stand around on windy street corners, he explained, and therefore in that mild climate he didn't need one.

He was something of a radical in the matter of clothing, yet it is a fact that the climate is singularly equable, and so it is along the coast of the entire state. Even though the northern extremity of California is in the latitude of Boston and its southern end is opposite Charleston, the thermometer seldom anywhere drops below freezing or rises to what is often experienced in New York City by the end of May. The breezes from the Pacific keep the land cool in summer and warm in winter.

Note:

The visitor to San Diego can choose among numberless hotels, from the most modest to the most palatial; or, if he prefers, can camp on Coronado Beach. The climate is unfailingly gentle, and the ocean and fertile valleys and distant mountains furnish many attractions. Most points of interest are easily accessible, and the traveler with limited time can see much in a very few days. There is excellent fishing and bathing. The glimpse of Mexico one gets at Tia Juana should not be missed, nor the ancient Mission and its olive trees, nor the adobe homes in "Old Town," nor the caverned cliffs at La Jolla.

A RUSTIC VILLAGE

Not for a long time had I been in a place that so filled me with delight as did Capistrano in Southern California. Such a dreamy, easy-going community— no hurry, no worry—such a luxuriant valley, such lofty environing hills with the green turf clothing every rounded outline! Then, to the north, were the rocky peaks of a mountain range, serene and blue in the distance. The village itself was a queer huddle of primitive houses, some no more than board shanties, and none of them large or in the least pretentious. However, the feature that gave especial distinction to the hamlet was the ruin of an old Mission, still impressive, calm and beautiful, and appealing powerfully to the imagination. It would interest one anywhere, and we can boast of so few ruins that have age and noble proportions in this new land of ours that the appeal was doubly strong. Though the Mission buildings are much shattered, some parts continue in use even to this day. The chime of four bells performs its accustomed service, one portion is used as a church, and there is a fine corridor in an excellent state of preservation.

The structures were begun in 1776. Adobe was

largely used for the walls, but the church was of stone with a lofty tower and a roof made of solid concrete domes. At early mass on Christmas morning in 1812 there was an earthquake that toppled over the tower onto the body of the building, and the entire roof crashed down. Forty-nine people were killed. "We've had no earthquake worth mentioning since," one of the leading Americans of the vicinity informed me. "Of course there have been a good many tremors, but they

have been mere sardines compared with that shock of 1812, and we pay no more attention to them than we would to a spatter of rain."

The village was charmingly pastoral. The insects thrummed, the children laughed and called at their play, the roosters crowed in endless succession, the dogs barked, and the cattle lowed from the luscious hillslopes. And what throngs of birds there were! I saw them flitting everywhere and the air was a-thrill with their songs. The mocking-birds were lilting their varied notes, the turtle-doves sounded their mellow calls, and in the vicinity of the buildings were multitudes of linnets—pretty little birds and cheerful songsters, but very destructive to grapes, apricots, peaches, pears and berries. In the pastures the red-winged blackbirds abounded, hovering about the sheep and cattle. Often they could be seen on the sheep's backs picking off ticks. Meadowlarks were frequently within sight and hearing, but their song was decidedly coarser and less plaintive than in the East. I observed many gay little birds known as "canaries," and there were flickers and pewees and bee-martins and thrashers and numerous others. Of them all I perhaps most enjoyed the swallows. A few had been noticed flying about for a week or two, but the mass of them had come the evening before I arrived. Now they were darting everywhere, building under the eaves of the houses and barns and establishing a populous colony beneath the loftiest cornice of the old Mission ruin. Far up against the blue sky I would sometimes see the buzzards soaring. Nothing in the way of offal escapes their alert eyes or scent. Back in the hills, if a man killed a gopher or a rattlesnake or some such little creature, there might not be a buzzard in sight at the time, but the next day half a dozen would be around.

On the noon that I reached Capistrano the main street was full of teams tied to the wayside hitching rails, and yet the place seemed mysteriously devoid of human beings. At last I discovered the male inhabitants of the region gathered at the far end of the street in and about an adobe Justice Court. The wide doorway was jammed full of men peering over each other's shoulders, and the case was evidently of the most absorbing and vital interest. At length, however, the gathering broke up, the village became populous, and one after another the teams were unhitched and driven away. The excitement, it seemed, concerned two individuals, one of whom had said the other was a liar, and the latter had responded that the former was a son of a gun and likened him to a variety of similar obnoxious things. But the court failed to get together a jury and the judge had dismissed the case. As a clerk in a local store expressed it, "The two fellers remind me of my schooldays when one of us kids'd sometimes go and complain to the teacher saying, 'Jimmy's been a-callin' me names.' "

" 'What's he been callin' you?' she asks him."

" 'I don't like to tell you,' the boy says, 'It's awful bad things.' "

While I was in this store, a fat old Indian entered. He had short hair, wore overalls, and except for his color was not much different in dress and appearance from a white workingman.

His breath was odorous of liquor, and he was loquacious and happy. The clerk introduced him as the best sheep-shearer in the county. He shook hands and said, "Me good man! You good man?"

In talking with him it was not easy to catch the meaning of some of his remarks. The common patois of the region used by both the whites and the darker skinned folk is based on Spanish, but with an intermixture of Indian and of words borrowed from the English. The old sheep-shearer had about fifty other Indians working under him in the season, got five dollars a day himself and two dollars for his wife who did the cooking for the gang. The wealth he acquired did not stick to him. He gambled it away.

Gambling was a common recreation among the villagers, and the place supported four "blind pigs," or unlicensed saloons. There were always loafers hanging about their porches and a noisy crowd inside playing pool. One of the Capistrano experts at poker was a Chinaman who had a ranch just outside the village. He lived in a dirty little hut there and kept his horse under a pepper tree with only the shelter afforded by the leafage. For ten miles around the people depended on him to supply them with vegetables. Some of the poorest families in the village bought of him rather than take the trouble to raise their own vegetables, though they have the finest kind of land right at their doors. "He can't hardly speak three words of English," I was told, "but he'll sit down and play poker all right with any of us. Perhaps he'll lose fifty dollars or more in a single sitting and not go home till the small hours of the morning, and yet he'll be at his work that day as usual without batting an eye. No doubt, on the whole, he makes oftener than he loses."

One of my acquaintances was a short, stooping old German with a broken nose. He lived in an adobe house with walls two or three feet thick. "You keep der adobe dry," said he, "und it vill last forever, but der vather from der eaves spatters oop und vashes avay der bottom till it breaks down unless you be careful. Some puts on cement to make der valls look nice und last more long. We do not build adobe houses now. It is quicker to use boards, und you cannot keep them so clean as a board house, und the air is not so goot inside. Some of der adobe houses are one hundred years old already, I tink. I haf not lif here always. My business is a bee ranch, twelve miles back in der hills. My home vas out dere till der dry years make me move. If you git no rain dere be no flowers—no not'ing. Perhaps der bees can find enough to keep alive, bud dere is no vork you can do to help. Der vather give out und everyt'ing, und you might as vell come avay. Last year it vas goot all right, und I t'ink dis year be good. So I soon shall haf to go dere. Dem hills are chock full o' flowers now— oh, yes—like a flower garden. I haf not been dere since last August. In another month the bees begin to swarm, und I haf to get ready for dot. You haf to be on der vatch or der swarms go avay; ish not often dey vill go into another hive demselves. Dey come out und hang on a bush while der scouts are lookin' for a goot place. Maybe a place is found und dey be off in one half hour. Maybe dey hang on der bush two, three day or a veek.

"Many time we haf bees fly over dis town. Perhaps dey stop und someone catch und put dem in an old box, und dey make honey. Bud der honey ish not much goot. Der flowers down here are not like dose on der hills. Here der country soon be yellow mit wild mustard, und dat make der honey a bitter taste und catch in your throat, just like as if you eat too much pepper. You couldn't sell it. Sometimes a swarm vill get in a house. It vill go in a crack, und perhaps der bees vill make honey in der ceiling, und it vill begin to leak through. Den der people haf to tear a hole und drive der bees out.

"Der honey in der hills is white as vather. Der bees haf hundreds of kind of flowers dere, but der best is der sagebrush. I wear a veil when I handle der bees und

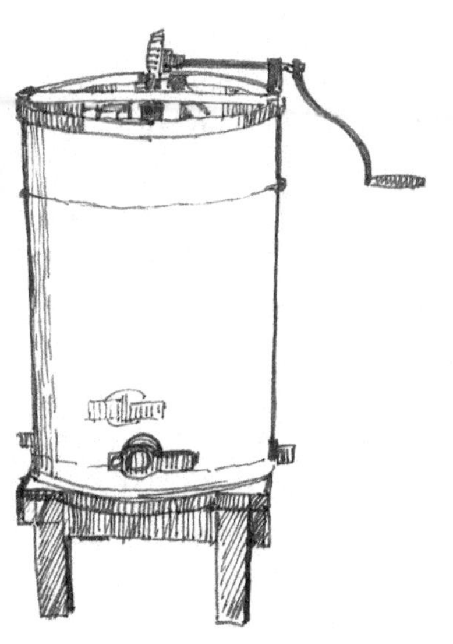

gloves mitout fingers. You cannot tell ven der bees vill sting—some days not at all, und other days dey joost like bulldogs. Dey sting ven dey feels like it, according to der veather.

"Each hive of bees vill make from one hundred to five hundred pounds of honey in a goot season, und I get about thirty tons from my two hundred stands. Der bees fill der frames each season half a dozen times. We extract der honey by puttin' der frames in a machine dat whirls dem and throws der honey out, bud leaves der comb to be put back in der hives. Dis vay der bees are save much vork, und dey get twice der honey dey used to did. In July, already you can do not'ing any more. Der best flowers are past und things are getting dry und der bees can only make what dey need demselves."

We were sitting on the post office piazza, and here we were joined just then by a man who was a former resident of the village and had recently arrived for a visit. He accosted my companion and they were soon discussing incidents of the past. Among other things they mentioned cock fights, and the German said, "Eighteen or nineteen years ago dey use to haf a cock fight mos' every Sunday, but I didn't see him now for a long time."

When the newcomer moved on, the German happened to turn his eyes toward home and remarked, "I haf now to go to my house. Dere is a peacock from my neighbor dot I can see on der roof. Sometime it vill stay dere all der night and holler; so I vill drive it off."

The peacock belonged on a place that formerly was the home of Don Foster, the feudal lord of the region. He had hundreds of thousands of acres, and sheep and cattle unnumbered, and he set a generous table free to all comers. Indeed, two or three dozen of the villagers were constantly fed at his board and he really supported "the whole shooting match" for they did practically no work.

The most exciting period in the village history

was that immediately following the acquisition of California by the Americans. To quote a leading citizen, "There was then a band of sixty or seventy disgruntled Mexicans known as 'Manillas' who were a terror to all the region. They had a leader by the name of Basquez who was credited with all sorts of savagery and wild escapades. He delighted to come unexpectedly when a dance was in progress and join in the merry-making and cut the fandango. Then, again, he would dash into a village with all his troop and commence firing. At once there'd be a yell, 'Basquez is in town!' and you'd ought to see the people hide.

"The Manillas sailed in here one day and captured the town, all except Don Foster's house. There's one old man living in Capistrano now who at the time of that raid had a store here. When they broke into his place he crawled under a big basket among some rags and rubbish in a corner. He heard the Mexicans helping themselves to his firearms and nice things, but he kept quiet and as soon as it was night he escaped to Don Foster's. After about a week the Manillas got news that the sheriff was comin' with a posse from Los Angeles to punish them, and they went and bush-whacked him and killed all but one man. The sheriff made a brave fight, and as he lay dying he kept firing his pistol at the fellows as long as he could hold it.

"In a short time another and bigger posse was gathered. Then the Mexicans scattered, but within a few months they'd nearly all been hunted down. When one was caught, there were no legal proceedings. He was just hung to a sycamore tree, or stood up against an adobe wall and shot. Last of all they waylaid Basquez and shot him all to pieces.

"This was a much bigger place years ago. In 1870 there were nearly two thousand inhabitants. Now there are less than four hundred. But in those days, they were practically all Mexicans and Indians who lived a subsistence existence. A few watermelons and a sack or two of beans will suffice a Mexican family for a year; they live from hand to mouth. Why, an energetic American will raise a crop of walnuts and clear in a single season four or five thousand dollars, which is more than a Mexican would clear in four or five thousand years.

"Most of the Indians have drifted off to the reservations to get the benefits from Uncle Sam. We've managed to pauperize nearly the whole race. If someone else will support them, they quit doing anything for themselves and are just loafers. As for the Mexicans, they were never reconciled to the change of government, and when there come a mining excitement down in their home country many of them went there and never returned. In spite of the decrease of numbers, we really get more out of the land than ever before. Nevertheless, there's plenty of laziness still. Work is plenty and men can earn a dollar and a half a day, but if they take a job they soon are tired or get too much money and lay off. A Mexican with five dollars will spend it like a lord. He is very apt to get drunk on Saturday night, and you never know whether he will be back to his work Monday morning or not. Some families are so shiftless we are obliged to support 'em. The county allows such from five to ten dollars a month. But they don't consider themselves indigents. They are, rather, indignants. We have no paupers. They call themselves 'pensioners' and think it an honor to get public aid."

English walnut growing had chief place among the local industries, and there were a number of extensive groves. The trees spread out like apple trees, but have a smooth light-gray bark. In the walnut harvest-time the school closes for six weeks to give the children a chance to help gather the crop. Some of the nuts fall of themselves, but a large proportion are thrashed off with poles. Often the poles have a hook on the end and by their aid the branches are shaken. The ground is free from weeds and has been gone over with a smoother so that the picking up is easy. A sack is the usual receptacle, but the women use their aprons. The nuts are spread on big racks to dry, where they are stirred once in a while with a garden rake. In two days of clear warm weather they are ready to ship.

There were a number of the great slatted drying benches in a yard back of my hotel. A few nuts were still left on the frames, and I often loitered there and feasted. If I chose I could supplement the nuts with oranges picked from trees in the garden. The hotel was an old-time stage-route tavern—a big, long two-story building with a piazza and balcony on both front and rear. I had to go upstairs outside and walk along the balcony to get to my room, which was a rather bare and shabby apartment, with a bed that had two boxes under it to prop up the slats. "We had a heavy-weight sleeping in your bed last night," explained the landlord, "and he broke through."

Behind the hotel were all sorts of whitewashed barns and sheds and shacks, including a kitchen and dining-room which were under a roof by themselves. Suspended from a full-foliaged pepper tree was a framework box covered with fly-netting. This served for a refrigerator. Among the various lodgers at the hotel when I arrived were three men who were driving a couple of wagons to San Diego. They had been stopping four days on account of rains that had flooded the rivers. There were no bridges, and the quicksands at the fords were treacherous. That evening one of the men came into the office and sat down on the counter. The landlord entered soon after, and he too roosted on the counter.

"What was that noise I heard as I passed through the yard?" asked the traveller. "It was in your barn, and, by gee! I thought it was snoring."

"That's what it was," replied the landlord. "It was my old black horse. He can snore to beat the band. He lies down flat with his head stretched out on the ground, and at it he goes. You punch him to wake him up and he grunts just like a person that's dead tired. He's the darndest horse I ever see."

"Well," said the traveller, "my father used to have a pair of horses that was great hands for sugar. When we got 'em out to go anywhere they wouldn't start unless we give 'em each a lump of sugar. Without that you couldn't get 'em to budge—not to save your neck from the rope. Those horses was a cute pair. One time some of us young fellers took 'em and drove to the beach for a picnic. We left 'em on a hill not far from the shore tied to the wagon, one on each side. Then we went down to the sea and fooled around and had a swim, and by the time we clumb back up the hill we was hungry as wolves. We'd left our lunch in the back end of the wagon. It was in a handle basket that had a lid flopping up from either way and, sir, those horses had got the covers up, one workin' on this side, one on that, and eaten every blessed thing, pie and all. My, wa'n't we mad! We made 'em pay for their grub though by running 'em home, seven miles in thirty minutes."

"You've decided to leave tomorrow, have you?" said the landlord.

"Yes," answered the other, "and I'd have gone before if we hadn't been drivin' mules. A horse with a load stuck in a quicksand will try its best to struggle out, but a mule will just lie down, and as soon as a mule's ears get full of water there's no saving him. He'll drown in spite of all you can do."

In response to some questions of mine the landlord became reminiscent. "My people come here in 1870," said he, "about fifteen years before the railroad was built, and papa bought the store which is now the hotel office. Capistrano was on the main route north and south, but there was no place in town where travellers could stay. They used to bother papa asking for accommodations, and finally he built on to the old store and made this big two-story hotel, and by golly, in those days it was jammed all the time. The stable was full too, and we kept a regular hostler. From the stable alone we took in nearly a thousand dollars a month. The daily stages, one going south, one going north, met here at midnight, and we always had hot coffee ready for persons that wanted it. You've noticed how the village people go and hang around the depot to see the trains come in. Well, they used to gather at our hotel just as thick to see those midnight stages arrive. The building of the railroad made a great sensation in the town. When the first engine poked her nose in sight a good many of the people fled to their homes and buried themselves under the bed-clothes. It was weeks before some of 'em would come out of their rooms, and there's those here today that you could no more get on a train than you could get them to fly. If they have to

go to Santa Ana, twenty-five miles away, they'll squat in the back end of a lumber wagon and jolt along that fashion rather than trust themselves to the train.

"This was a rough town in the old days. Behind the counter in our store we had a pistol every few feet to be ready for emergencies. We ran a bar in connection with the store, and one day an Indian come in and wanted liquor. He was drunk already, and I told him he couldn't have any more. That didn't suit him and he drew a knife on me. I picked up a pistol and gave him a welt with the butt that laid him flat on his back. Then I took him by the heels and dragged him out into the street. I thought he was dead, but pretty soon he drew up first one foot and then the other. After that he tried to sit up, but he'd roll over back on the ground. At last, however, he made out to crawl away.

"Papa had almost the same experience with a Mexican. The fellow stooped down and took from his bootleg a knife eighteen inches long and sharpened on both edges. But while he was stooping papa got a couple of pistols and poked 'em into his face as he looked up and said, 'You give me that knife or I'll blow the top of your head off.'

" 'Boss, don't shoot,' the fellow said, and he laid down the knife.

"I'm goin' to take that knife up to Los Angeles,' papa told him, 'and leave it and your name with the sheriff, and the next time you don't behave they'll come down here and kill you.'

"The Mexican was scared. 'Don't do that, boss,' he begged. 'You give me back my knife, and I'll work for you as long as you want.'

"So finally papa give him the knife, and after that the Mexican was his best friend. There was nothing the fellow wouldn't do for him.

"You ought to be here the last day of Lent—Judas Day, we call it. The night before, it is customary for the Mexicans to ransack the village and steal buggies and tools and anything they can carry off, and they make a big pile of all this plunder just outside the fence in front of the old Mission. Then they take a worn-out suit of clothes and stuff it full of weeds and stick it up on top of the pile, and that is Judas. Next they get an old dress and stuff that full of weeds and set it up side of Judas to represent his wife. In the morning when we wake up we find all the vehicles and loose things that were around our yards stacked up over by the Mission, with those two scarecrow figures on top. But the best of the performance comes in the afternoon when the Mexicans bring to the village two half-wild bulls from the hills. They tie Judas to one and Judas's wife to the other and chase the creatures up and down the street till the two figures are torn to tatters.

"There was one Judas Day a tramp come to town, and he stopped at the store and bought a couple of dozen eggs. As he was goin' out of the door carryin' the eggs in a bucket papa says to him, 'They're just turnin' the bulls loose out there, and you'd better wait a while.'

"But he said he was in a hurry and he wouldn't stop. We watched him, and about the time he got in the middle of the street one of the bulls come tearin' along and hits him in the seat of the pants. He went one way and his eggs went another, and that would have been the end of him if the vaqueros hadn't galloped to his rescue. He was mad and he went to Judge Bacon's office and said, 'I want to have these fellows out here arrested. They've been lettin' wild and vicious animals loose in the street and I've been knocked down, and two dozen eggs I'd just bought are all smashed.'

" 'Well,' the Judge said, 'I don't like to arrest these men. This is an annual celebration, and the men themselves didn't do the damage. If anyone is to be arrested it ought to be the bull.'

" 'I don't care who or what it is you arrest,' the tramp said; 'I want justice done.'

" 'Don't bother me any longer,' the Judge said, and he pulled out a dollar. 'Here, take this and go buy some more eggs,' said he.

"So the fellow left satisfied."

The traveller sitting beside the landlord now got down off the counter and stretched himself. "Who was the man that was here to dinner and went away just afterward on the train?" he inquired.

"It was a doctor," the landlord replied. "He had some thought of settling here, but I told him he'd starve to death. You see the people avoid callin' a doctor till the sick person has one foot in the grave and the other following after. The old women think they can cure most anyone with herbs and weeds, and they keep dosing the sick person till he's nearly dead. Then if the doctor can pull him through things are all right, but if the doctor has his patient die on him they'll never pay for his services.

"Whenever there's a death, whether it is day or night, the first thing that is done is to make a run for the Mission to toll the bells. They toll the two big ones for a grown person and the two little ones for a child. The bells toll for ten minutes, and all the friends and relatives start for the house of mourning—get up out of their beds to go, if it is night. The corpse is dressed in what had been the deceased's best clothes and is put on a table, and candles are lighted and set about on the table and outside on the porch. When all this has been done, the company kneel and sing a hymn. Each new arrival who comes later kneels by the body and says a prayer, and some of the women are praying pretty constantly. A crowd is hanging around all the time till after the funeral.

"On the day of the death, or the one following, some of the men go up to the cemetery to dig the grave, but they have a big demijohn of wine with them and they're sure to quit when they've got down about three feet. The next night there is a wake and a feast. It is the fashion to eat, drink and be merry and fight. If the night is cool the men and boys build a fire outside which they gather around. By three or four in the morning they are ready to scrap. They are full of their cheap wine then, and it don't require much to stir their anger.

"The morning after the wake, at ten o'clock, the bell begins to toll for the funeral and the grave-diggers hustle off to finish their work. An hour later the funeral takes place. The coffin is usually an ordinary box made in the village and covered with black cloth for an adult, white for a child. On the cloth are fastened many flowers and crosses and other figures made out of tissue and gold papers. The coffin is carried on men's shoulders to the church where the people sing a hymn and then go to the grave bearing the coffin in relays. At the cemetery, they sing again and recite a prayer. Lastly the body is lowered into the grave and every man, woman and child tosses in a handful of dirt."

For twenty-five dollars, a family can have a priest conduct the funeral, and while he goes through the sacred rites, the coffin reposes on a table in the church. For fifty dollars, a more elaborate service can be had, and the coffin rests on two tables, one placed on the other, while for seventy-five dollars the coffin has three tables beneath and the priest puts on his full robes, swings the censer, brings forth the silver candlesticks and makes the ceremony superlatively impressive.

Weddings take place at the church at high noon, and the rest of the day and the night till broad daylight is spent in feasting and dancing and in eating a barbecued beef.

A christening is also an occasion for "a big blowout." It takes place on Sunday, of course, and outside of the Mission in the churchyard is a crowd of men and boys who, as soon as the christening party comes forth, begin to shout and fire pistols and guns, and they follow the party home banging away as they go.

An Eastern girl, not long before, had told me something of her experience as a school teacher in San Diego County. She was twenty miles back from the railroad among the hills. The people were Americans, but they were shiftless and ignorant, and the women and children did most of the work. The man at the place where she boarded was a fair sample of what the other men were. He did not drink or smoke and was in no wise vicious, but he didn't amount to anything. The woman and her children looked after the garden, took care of the cows, raised the chickens, harvested the crops, and brought the house water from a spring a half mile distant. The older girls, when they came from school, would put on overalls and milk the cows. Often the children were dismissed from school to run the mowing-machine and get in the oats and barley which were raised for hay. The woman would even go and dig greasewood roots which they cut up for household fuel. Sometimes she would get ready a load of the roots, and the man would take the load to the nearest town to sell. He occasionally did a little ploughing, but he would exert himself most in

hunting wild bees that had made their homes in the hollow oaks.

There was no feminine timidity in that region. The girls were ready to kill rattlesnakes as often as they encountered them and all the women could shoot. Every few days the teacher's landlady went out with her gun and would return with five or six rabbits.

The children were all apt to be at school regularly, but this was because short attendance would mean a curtailing of the school money. The parents, however, were not at all particular to have their progeny there on time, or to have them stay the sessions out. Still, they preferred a clean record, and in order that the children should not be marked tardy, they requested the teacher to turn the clock back an hour or so in the morning. Their previous teacher had done this, they said. The pupils were very docile and patient. They seemed not to have life enough to be mischievous, and they could be kept on the same lesson for two weeks and never utter a complaint. Indeed, they would study it just as faithfully at the end of that period as at the beginning.

This glimpse of educational conditions stimulated a desire to visit the school at Capistrano. I found about seventy-five children in two rooms, the little ones under a young woman, the upper grades under a young man. They were an odd mixture, whites and Mexicans and Indians, and various combinations of the races.

Many of the children have only a vague understanding of English, and this makes their progress in school doubly slow. The building and its surroundings and the two teachers were all that could be desired. A generation ago the place had no school, but one day a New England resident of the village stumbled on the fact that they could get money from the state for educational purposes. This man was the local Justice of the Peace and known as Judge Bacon. "The people here didn't want to learn anything," said one of the early settlers in telling me the story, "and if a school of the usual sort had been established they wouldn't have attended. They'd heard of such a thing as a public school, but they didn't really know what it was. Why, these billy-goats had the idea it was a sort of institution to make Protestants out of 'em. To get around that snag Bacon went to the padre and asked him to start the school and teach it himself in his little rooms at the old Mission.

"Well, the padre couldn't spell one syllable of English, but Bacon got him to undertake the job, and dug up a diploma from somewhere allowing him to accept the position. The children came, and he kept along and kept along for a year or so. Most of the school conversation was in the Spanish language, and what was learned didn't amount to much, but it was a start and about the only way a school here could start. However, at the end of a year Bacon persuaded the padre that teaching school was beneath the dignity of a Catholic priest and fixed things so the priest was authorized to hire a nice young lady to take his place. He got one and she taught about three months, when we had a horse race here and some feller came along and made love to her. The result was she ran away with him, and gad! we've never seen her since.

"The school was Bacon's hobby, and he got a building put up and afterward painted it himself—spent three weeks at the job. He laid out the grounds around with the notion of having a sort of park, and he urged that there should be put on the post at each corner of the fence a big globe having the entire world mapped on it. Then, inside, on an arch over the teacher's alcove he wanted a motto painted—'The poorest child may tread the classic halls of yore.' But there were two other trustees, and we wouldn't agree to these things. We didn't see much sense to 'the classic halls of yore,' and were afraid it would only get us laughed at. So, instead, we finally had an eagle and some stars painted on the arch.

"Bacon knew how to read and write, but that was about the extent of his book learning. He was one of the argonauts of '49. He made money in mines and then he invested in cattle here. His home was an old adobe without a floor, but he was rich—oh, heavens! he had money galore. As soon as he got the school building done, he put in a seventy-five-dollar chandelier to light up so they could have dances. He paid for it—plunked up every nickel himself, and he furnished the oil, and he hired a dancing master to come from Los Angeles. They had a dance every Wednesday night. One day he says to a mother, 'Why wasn't your girl there last time?'

" 'She can't go no more,' the mother says. 'She's just wearin' out her Sunday gaiters on the floor there, and I can't have it.'

" 'Buy her a pair of gaiters, and I'll pay for 'em,' says he, and after that he had to buy gaiters for every girl in town, you bet-cher!

"In fact he got into the habit of buying anything the girls said they wanted for the dancing. But after a while they carried matters a little too far. I remember how he called on me and said, 'One of my best dancers that lives down here on the lane has balked.'

" 'What has she balked for?' I asked.

" 'Well,' he replies, 'she says she's got no corsets. Now I've give them girls calico frocks and shoes and lots of things, but I've got to draw the line somewhere, and I won't give 'em corsets.'

"After that the weekly dance ran down. Then pretty soon the idea struck him he'd like to learn music. So he sent to Philadelphia for instruments to fit out a brass band, and he got the finest that money could buy. He distributed them among a lot of old pickles of his caliber, but I told him he'd forgot one thing—'Whoever heard of a brass band without a banjo?' I said.

"At once he telegraphed to have a banjo sent regardless of expense. Those old stiffs he picked out for members of the band knew no more about music than a dog does about his grandfather, but they went to practicing in a room here in the town and kept at it till the neighbors fired 'em out. Then they made their headquarters off a couple of miles on a sheep ranch where the coyotes were in the habit of gathering to serenade the ranch dwellers. They petered out after a while. The only fellow among them who pretended to do real well was the man with the bass drum. 'Oh, yes,' he'd say, 'I'm gettin' along first rate. All I have to do is to draw off once in a while and give her a devil of a whack!'

"Bacon was an old resident when I came, and he's been long dead. It was his habit every time he wanted to go away anywhere to buy two or three white shirts. When he'd worn 'em he'd chuck 'em in a closet and never bother with 'em again. After his death, when things was bein' settled up, we come across all that big heap of white shirts, and we threw 'em outside. The result was that every Mexican in the place wore a white shirt for the next few months."

Notes:

Capistrano is not a tourist resort, and its hotel accommodations are poor, yet this lack is not without certain picturesque compensations. The village is one of the quaintest, its setting among the hills is charming, and it has the most imposing and beautiful Mission ruin in California. No traveler who goes to San Diego can afford to miss visiting the place, if only to stop off from one train and go on by the next. The outlying sections of the village where the Indians and poorer inhabitants dwell should not be neglected, and it would be well to visit the wild, abrupt coast. This is close at hand and has an added interest because of the adventurous incidents which Dana in his *Two Years Before the Mast* describes as occurring in his experiences there.

About thirty miles south of Capistrano, and four miles from the railway station of Oceanside, is the San Luis Rey Mission, which, after being in ruins for nearly a century, is again occupied by monks.

There is an automobile route the entire distance from Los Angeles to San Diego, one hundred and thirty-six miles over roads that as a rule are good but have some bad sandy stretches.

SPRING IN SOUTHERN CALIFORNIA

One of my longest stops was at a private house well out in a suburban district of Los Angeles. From the window of my room I looked forth on a world luxuriantly green and brightened with blossoms in marvelous profusion. To add to the pleasure of all this, birds were plentiful and, in particular, there was a mockingbird that had a habit of perching not far away and piping and trilling with rare ardor and eloquence. Several palms, a magnolia and some camphor trees grew in front of the house, and behind it were orange, fig, peach and other fruit trees. The entire region was much like a park, so carefully were the orchards kept, and so abounding were the cultivated flowers and shrubs. The surroundings of the finer dwellings were little short of perfection, and there was never any rawness due to waiting for nature to give them a proper setting, even about the newer homes. Things grow so quickly and respond so readily to man's training that a home almost at once nestles in flowers and vines and foliage that give it repose and charm.

The story goes that the climate is so favoring you can plant toothpicks one day and the next morning find them grown into tall trees that can be cut and sold for telegraph poles. In sober fact, the nearest approach to this is the growth made by the blue gum, a species of eucalyptus. Aside from fruit trees, no trees in Southern California are so conspicuous and abundant. A blue

gum will send up a shoot twenty feet tall in a twelve-month; and in Australia, its home land, it attains a mature height of three hundred feet. The Californians usually cut their blue gums down every few years, and sprouts are allowed to start from the stump. "Our trees here don't know when they are dead," I was informed, "for no matter how little is left when the blue gums are chopped off they will at once take a new start as vigorous as ever. Why, a small patch of blue gums will keep a family in wood."

Throughout California, no matter where one wanders, mountains are always in sight glorifying every landscape. Where I then was I could see a series of heights close at hand, lofty and rugged. During the cooler months, the clouds love to linger about their summits and they often whiten over with snow, but no snow falls in the vale, though there are sometimes touches of frost. Things continue green and blossoms are profuse throughout the winter, and there is a gradual increase of color and fresh growth until high tide is reached in April. Then water is no longer so abundant, and presently the flowers go to seed and the grass withers, and except where there is irrigation the face of the earth is sere and sober. Thus it remains till late autumn when the reviving showers awaken the dull fields and roadsides and pastures to life.

The summer heat is at times excessive, yet it is a dry heat that does not carry with it a sweltering discomfort. What is far worse are the dust storms. In some sections these are frequent, and they are experienced occasionally even in Los Angeles. The dust fills the air like a fog and penetrates the houses and covers everything. Moreover, it irritates the throat and makes one constantly thirsty. Out on the desert, the wind, besides raising the dust, whirls the sand through the air, and sand-drifts gather in the lee of all obstructions. One man told me about an experience of his in a desert sand-storm in a top buggy. "The dusty wind had been blowing all day and night," said he, "and then let up. I'd been waiting for that and I started, but it had only quit to get a fresh hold and it soon blowed like the mischief again. The sand cut my face and the alkali in it made the tears run. Pretty soon my buggy blew over, but got it right side up again and went on. A little farther along it capsized once more, and this time the top blew off and went bounding away out of sight. The storm was so blinding I couldn't see a thing ten feet distant, and I'd been troubled a good deal to keep in the road because the wind was so fierce it would pull on the reins and get the horse out of the beaten track. So in making a new start I just tied the reins to the harness. Then I got into my wrecked buggy and let the horse find its own way home."

Evidently the California summer is not in some respects all it might be, and the winter also has its failings, though of a different sort. In a Chicago railway station, on my way from the East, I overheard an Ohio woman who was returning from a visit to the Pacific Coast discoursing on its weather to a chance acquaintance. Her voice was hoarse with a severe cold. "I've never seen worse fog anywhere," said she, "and the tourists were all kicking about it. I wasn't comfortably warm half the time, and I had to wear jis as heavy furs as at home. The houses ain't fixed to heat.

They don't have stoves except in their kitchens. So you can only sit around and shiver. Even in summer the nights are chilly, no matter how hot the day has been. You have to be careful not to let in too much of that night air or you'll ketch your death of cold. I've never minded the winter in Ohio half as much as I did this winter out there. Then, too, I've always been used to livin' at home, and though the grub was good I got tired of hotel cookin'. Of course, there's wonderful things to see and all that, and I was enjoying myself pretty well until I struck Los Angeles where I got this awful cold. I didn't meet any people there but jis had colds, and I heard a lot of tourists sayin' they wouldn't live there if you'd give 'em the finest house in the city. It seemed like I was never goin' to get over my cold, and I said, 'Ohio is good enough for me. I can die as well there as out here,' and now that I'm most back I'm so glad I don't know what to do."

No doubt her experience was in some respects abnormal. The season was an unusually wet one, and I witnessed several astonishing downpours when torrents brown with sediment flowed in every roadside gutter, and some of the streets were a-wash from curb to curb. The worst flooded ones could only be crossed by wading in water a foot or more deep. Often boards or pieces of timber were laid across the gutter streams to serve as makeshift bridges.

The uncommon wetness of the season was attributed by some people to the magic of a professional rainmaker. The previous year had been dry, and he contracted to bring rain by a certain date. Then he betook himself to a mountaintop, but what mysterious rites he performed in his efforts to produce rain no one knows. The desired result failed to materialize until two days after the time set, and for this reason payment was refused. The rainmaker, however, had his revenge by drenching the country at frequent intervals, and in some sections there were disastrous floods. He declared he would

not desist until he was paid. Thus urged, his employers finally turned over the money, and the torrential rains more or less promptly ceased.

Probably the most delightful excursion that can be made from Los Angeles is to the island of Santa Catalina, twenty-five miles off the coast. When first discovered the island was thickly populated by Indians, and later it was frequented by pirates who preyed on the rich galleons in the Philippine trade. Now it is a pleasure resort that attracts multitudes of visitors, and its single village is a crowded settlement of hotels and shops and numerous little cottages huddled in a narrow valley basin. Thence you look forth on a crescent beach with wave-torn bluffs on either side reaching out into the sea. In all its length of twenty miles and its width of from two to nine, the island is a chaos of steep hills and mountains, furrowed with deep canyons and having many rugged precipices. The loftiest height is Black Jack which rises twenty-five hundred feet above the sea level. Most of the slopes are grassed over, and thousands of sheep find pasturage on them. You see the paths of the grazing flocks everywhere winding along the inclines, and often see the sheep themselves or hear their bleating. Off in the middle of the island is a farmhouse where the caretakers of the flocks live, but otherwise human life is confined to the neighborhood of the village of the pleasure-seekers.

No matter whither I wandered I found a constant succession of glens and ridges clothed with scattered bushes and thorny clumps of cacti, and one can judge of the country inland by the fact that two young men who had lived in Santa Catalina for years recently lost themselves while coming from the west shore eight miles distant. A fog bewildered them, and one gave up with heart trouble or whiskey, and the other went on alone. Night came, and the wanderer stumbled about in the darkness all to no purpose. It was afternoon of the next day when he reached the village. Then search parties started to find his companion, but he was not where he had been left, and it was two days later that they came across him in a remote part of the island trying to find his way back to civilization.

The showers that every now and then trailed over the uplands and down into the vales were full of vague mystery. There was mystery too in the gray old ocean always pounding along the shore, and in the drift of sunlight and shadow across its sober expanse. I had one experience that seemed to argue that this poetic quality as evinced by nature had a marked influence on the island dwellers and made them poetic also. The first night at my hotel I was awakened early in the morning by voices under my room. Evidently the floor was thin and I was over the dining room. A waiter was giving his comrades some advice and it was in rhyme, as follows:

"Mary Ann was very good;
She always did the best she could.
Now children be like Mary Ann,
And do the very best you can."

A mile or two back from the village up a canyon lived an old hermit who had a chicken ranch. Any farm or country home with land attached, even if there is no more than a garden patch, is a "ranch" in California. I called on the hermit one day. His house was of the shanty order standing in the midst of a plot of ground which he had palisaded with a lath fence against his marauding fowls. Besides chickens he had hundreds of pigeons and a few ducks and turkeys. For closer companionship, he kept a couple of handsome collies, and when the sheep from the hills came down around his place, the dogs drove them back.

"I've been on Santa Catalina twenty years," said he. "It was just beginnin' to be a resort when I got here. There was one small hotel and a few boarding houses, and often more people would come than they could accommodate. Then a good many would have to sleep on the beach. Our summer weather is all right so they didn't suffer from damp or cold, but they did sometimes get into trouble with the sand fleas. We got fleas here pretty near as big as a grain of wheat, you bet!"

The hermit had a number of flourishing fig and peach trees and was starting some grapevines. I noticed several rank-growing plants I thought looked like tobacco. "That's what they are," said he. "One day an Irishman from Los Angeles called on me and he saw a chicken pickin' at itself, and he caught it and looked to see what was the matter. He found some mites, and he says, 'What little tej'ous things are these?'

"I told him, and said I could get rid of them if I had some tobacco leaves. Well, the next time he come he brought a packet of tobacco seed, and he said, 'You raise some tobacco and you use it on your chickens. If you don't I'll kill you.'

"It grows very good here. If you have water you can grow most anything in this soil except greenbacks. Would you like to see our island foxes? They're a sort you don't find on the mainland. I caught one last night in that box over there. I've heared him a-howlin' around for a week, and he got three chickens o' mine. These foxes make nice pets and I s'pose I've caught as many as four hundred and sold them at a dollar apiece."

We went to the box, and he tilted it up so that I could see the pretty creature within, evidently a fox but only half the mainland size. I believe the island contains certain other creatures with  a peculiar individuality, but it is especially famous for the fish in the surrounding sea. Here is found the leaping tuna, the most active game fish in the world. It is caught with a rod and line, but the line must be many hundreds of feet long, and the fish will tow the boat at racehorse speed from one to twenty miles before it is captured. In weight the tuna sometimes exceeds two hundred pounds.

Nothing afforded me quite so much pleasure while I was at the island as a trip in one of the glass-bottomed boats. The boat could have carried a score, but two young men in addition to myself were the only passengers this time. There was a continuous cushioned seat at the sides and stern, and the oarsman sat in the prow. We had an awning overhead, and in the bottom of the boat were three heavy plates of glass about eighteen inches by three feet, boxed in at the sides. The harbor water was somewhat roiled, but as soon as we got to the cliffs jutting seaward, we looked down into fairyland. Even when the depth was fully fifty feet there was scarcely any obscurity, and the sunbeams flickered down almost as through the air

onto the gray rocks and the wafting, many-hued sea-plants and the numerous finny inhabitants. How calm everything down there seemed! and with what lazy pleasure the fish moved about in their wonder-world! They were marvelously colored—red and blue, silver and brown, striped and spotted, and some were pallid little sardines just hatched, and others would weigh four or five pounds.

My fellow voyagers almost exhausted themselves in their expressions of delight. "Well, sir," one would cry, "this is the finest sight I've ever seen in my life."

Then the other would break in with, "Look at this gold fish! Ain't he a pippin! and Tom, here's a jelly fish right under the glass. Gee! ain't that pretty?"

"Dick, get onto this!" exclaims Tom. "Do you see the fish with spots on its back like lamps?"

"That's the electric fish," explained the oarsman, "and in the dark those spots light up the water. Now we are going over a lot of seaweed-ribbons and lace and such. It's the wet drygoods of the ocean, and there's enough right in sight to stock a millinery store."

"I s'pose you can catch fish here at the island any old place," remarked Tom. "My! it looks so nice down in there it would just suit me to camp under water right here for a while."

"Those gold fish take my eye," declared Dick. "I would certainly like to reach down and grab a couple."

"See that seaweed with the violet-colored tips," said Tom. "I tell you that's pretty."

"That was nice all right," agreed Dick, "but look at this big purple shell lying on the bottom. I wish I had it."

Just then a little rowboat approached in which were two fellows in bathing suits, and our oarsman spoke to Dick and said, "If you want that shell, one of those chaps will go down and get it for a quarter."

So the other boat was hailed and as soon as the diver had leaned over into our craft to take a look through the glass and locate the shell, down he went, and we could see him swimming like a frog straight for it. When he came up he gave a rap on the glass beneath us, and then he presented the shell, climbed into his boat and put an old coat about his shoulders. "There's a number of such divers here," said our rower as we moved away, "and they make big money—five, ten and twenty dollars a day, but they don't live long. If they ketch a cold it goes right to their lungs."

From Santa Catalina I returned to the mainland and went far back from the coast to a small isolated village. I arrived one warm noontide. A cow was wandering about the wide unshadowed main street, a few teams were hitched to wayside posts before the half dozen stores and saloons, and a rooster was scratching over a gutter rubbish heap. At one end of the street was a patch of grass and a group of trees, and here a prospector's outfit had stopped. The outfit consisted of a canvas-topped wagon loaded with supplies and drawn by four mules which were eating oats from their nose bags. On either side of the vehicle was a water barrel, and on behind a sheet-iron stove and a bale of hay. The proprietors were three men enroute for Death Valley, and they were prepared to spend a year searching for wealth in that desert region.

On the rear borders of the hamlet stood a tiny church with a barbed-wire fence around it. A preacher came from somewhere and held service every other Sunday. I was told that only two men in the place were church-goers and that the minister considered it was a big day if he had an audience of ten. Beyond the church were park-like pastures with frequent great oaks just putting forth their new foliage. But as a whole the surroundings were either level plains growing in their better parts to wheat and barley or were low parched hills thinly covered with sagebrush and mesquite.

The village was on the Newhall Ranch, which includes nearly fifty thousand acres. When "old man Newhall" was alive all the suitable land was in wheat, and at the time of harvest he often shipped several trainloads in a day, while now it is something notable to fill half a dozen cars in that time. The village was a busy place then, for not only were two or three score men employed on the ranch, but twice as many more were working some neighboring oil wells, now abandoned. A lanky long-haired youth who had charge of one of the drink resorts told me the history of the place while he sat on a battered and initial-carved settee in front of his saloon and contemplatively smoked a cigarette.

"Dad come here twenty odd years ago," he said, "and he's seen this town drop four times and the business go dead. Well, things are not so bad just now as they might be. We get the trade from the ranches for ten to thirty miles around, and they've been makin' somethin' the last few years and have money to spend. One while we lived in Los Angeles. That's quite a burg and gettin' bigger all the time. I used to could say nobody could lose me in Los Angeles, but I don't hardly know where I'm at in some parts now."

When I left the village to resume my journeyings, it so happened that I was stranded for several hours at a railway junction, a few miles distant, where I had to stay till midnight before I could get a train. One attraction of the waiting-room was a gambling-machine. You put a nickel in a slot, turned a crank and something went buzz inside, and possibly a sum varying from ten cents to two dollars dropped out down below. I saw a number of fellows try it, and two of them used up a quarter each in their efforts, but the machine simply kept what they dropped in and gave back no prizes. The profits of the machine, according to the man in charge of the station lunch counter, were about a dollar a day. He said the thing was against the law and would not be allowed in the cities, but in small places the law was not enforced.

The lunch man and a friend had a long discussion about the merits of various systems of gambling—cards, craps, roulette and faro bank—and attempted to decide which was "the fairest game in the bunch." "I've tried them all," said the friend. "Yes, I've monkeyed around the gambling tables a good deal. I am naturally lucky, too, and when I win, I win right quick."

Nevertheless, he was at present so hard up he was planning to beat his way on a frieght to some land of promise farther on. He went out, and the lunch man turned to me and said, "There ain't much use of playin' against a professional gambler. He ain't settin' there for his health, and he's bound to win oftener'n you are. But a feller knockin' about always sees ways to make a lot of money if he only had a little pile. It takes too long and requires too much effort to earn and save it. So he tries gambling, and yet if he has luck he always wants more money than he has won, and he won't stop until he loses it all.

"Some of the worst gambling places are over in Arizona. I went into one town there with fifty bucks (dollars) in my pocket and wearin' a twenty-eight-dollar suit and a new overcoat and shoes, and with a four-dollar grip in my hand. But in three weeks I come away a tramp. Now I've made up my mind to do different," said he as he prepared a cup of coffee for himself. "I ain't touched my booze for a month, and if I can save seventy-five dollars, I'm goin' to start for New England where I come from. I can have more fun with five dollars in Boston than I can with a hundred dollars in these cities out here."

Most likely he would fail in his intention. The Far West is full of human driftwood. Men who have any capacity and industry easily get profitable jobs, but a considerable proportion of such men are constantly roving to new territory, and money doesn't stick to them.

My midnight train carried me to the remarkably fertile country that extends for nearly a hundred miles east of Los Angeles. There you find an endless succession of orange, lemon, apricot, peach and other fruit orchards. Back a little from the route I took through this wonderland, the mountains frowned in purple gloom from

beneath a capping of foggy clouds, and wherever a canyon opened from the heights it had shot out over the levels a wide waste of sand and stones that was half overgrown with brush. Such land was furrowed with water-courses that were perfectly dry except just after storms. However, dry water-courses are not confined in California to small streams. There is a saying that the rivers are "bottom upward." That is, the channel is usually a waste of sand, but if you dig down deep enough you are pretty sure to find a seepage of water. After a storm, the dry channels are suddenly filled with rushing torrents that transform the lowlands to shallow ponds and marshes of mire.

In the region where I then was oranges grow to perfection, but they are raised with scarcely less success in the upper Sacramento valley over five hundred miles to the north. Heat and cold on the coast are a matter of altitude, not latitude, and the wildflowers are a-bloom among the foothills and the valleys in midwinter throughout the entire length of the state. What wonder that California is the great orange center of the world!

With proper care the trees grow very rapidly. They are vigorous and long-lived. For a hundred years, they will continue to bear, and an instance is on record in Italy of an orange tree that survived to the age of four centuries. Perhaps no other tree blossoms more regularly and generously, and though sometimes a cold wave does serious local harm, a general failure of the crop is unknown. The trees require little or no pruning back, but the branches have to be thinned out somewhat. To combat the scale pests a good many owners resort to spraying, but the most effective way is to fumigate. The leading varieties of trees only grow about ten feet high and are very compact with branches trailing on the ground. Even the larger species seldom attain over fifteen feet, so that a tent can be put over a tree and the fumigating done very thoroughly. Tents enough are used to cover a row, and when that row has been treated they are shifted to the next. It is night work for the heat of the day and the fumes combined would injure the foliage.

In the early spring one finds much of the land among the orange groves hidden by rank weeds, and by peas purposely grown during the winter and later ploughed under to serve as a fertilizer and to give the soil humus. After the ploughing the land is kept clean, and it is cultivated many times in the months following. The bare brown earth is not a pleasing setting for the evergreen, glossy-foliaged trees, and their appeal to the eye is also hurt by the round, stout solidity and uniformity of shape of the trees themselves.

Picking begins in time to ship for Thanksgiving use, but the early fruit is poor. It is not ripe, and in order to get a good outer color some of it has to be treated to a few days' sweat. This turns a green skin to the proper tint, though the inside may be as sour as a lemon. The picking continues until May, and in the height of the season you can buy excellent windfalls from peddlers on the town streets at "ten cents a bucket," and the bucket holds about eight quarts.

A well-grown orchard, conveniently located, is commonly priced at fifteen hundred to two thousand dollars an acre, though at such figures the native Californians, if they give you a confidential opinion, say they don't see how any money can be made. It is better to sacrifice something on location, for the investment will be decidedly less. There is great advantage to a prospective purchaser in working in the country a year or two in order to get acquainted with the climate, the soil and crops and methods of marketing. The tenderfoot usually pays high for the place he buys, and often he "comes with a nice little pile and goes back with nothing." Many natives make a business of staying on a place for a while, improving it and then selling at a fancy valuation. That done, they buy some other ranch, which can be had cheap, and repeat the process.

The manipulations that one hears of in connection with the sale of land in the coast country make a very curious story. The real estate agents are persons of an optimistic turn of mind, with a marked ability to tell fairy tales. I heard of one man who was dissatisfied with the place he owned, and he put it in the hands of a firm of agents to sell while he looked up another home to his liking. Shortly afterward he saw a place advertised by these agents that he felt from the description was exactly the thing he wanted. He went to them, and lo! it was the very one he was trying to sell.

The agents are all eager to get hold of prospective purchasers, and some of the loiterers at the station are likely to be acting in their interest. That old Kansas farmer you see chewing tobacco and sitting around in the waiting room is wintering in the vicinity, and he is making a little money by keeping on the lookout for new arrivals, getting acquainted with them, and if they want to buy land he steers them to some real estate firm with which he has an understanding.

Everybody trades in land "on the side," even cheap clerks and servant girls. They can get lots for one dollar down and a dollar a week. But most of the small speculators pay in cash one-fourth of the price and agree to pay the other quarters at six month intervals. They really never intend to make the second payment, but expect the land to advance in value so they can sell out at a good profit before the six months expire. In short, they seldom buy because they want the property for themselves but simply to await some bigger "sucker" who will take it off their hands at an advance. With prices going up the investors generally make money. On the other hand, a drop in values finds a vast number of obligations that cannot be taken care of. The speculators are forced to sell for what they can get, which makes prices tumble still worse and there is a general crash. The preceding inflation has often been so great that it is difficult to estimate what a person has really dropped. "I have lost fifty thousand dollars," said one investor, "and the worst of it is that five hundred dollars of the sum was good money."

One real estate agent who talked to me with unusual frankness was a man who had just retired from the business after a ten months' experience. He had come from South Dakota and had made his home in a growing coast city of ten thousand inhabitants. "I have been successful," said he, "but my Godfrey! I didn't feel right. You can't tell the whole truth and make any sales. Southern California is a good place to spend money and a poor place to make it. For some people it's healthy, but for me the winters are too damp and chilly, and yet the natives say you don't need no fire. The fact is, fuel is expensive and most people can't afford it. There's many a family makes one cord of wood last a whole year, but I burned just as much as we did at home in the East.

"A considerable number of widows lived in the town where I was. When a woman had a little money left at her husband's death she'd buy or build a nice-looking house, but if you examined it you'd find it was put up very slight and cheap. Outside there'd be clapboards nailed right to the studding, and inside cheese cloth over lath and wall paper pasted on the cloth. The place was a summer resort, and for three or four months the lone woman with a house would rent her dwelling and live herself in a tent or shed behind it. The money she received had to support her the year through. So her food was mostly bread and a little fish and tea, with now and then five cents worth of warm soup bought at a restaurant. All the time she'd put on the appearance of being very well off, though in reality she was poorer than Job's turkey.

"People in the East think that the climate in

California is so favorable that they can pay any price for a ranch and make money on whatever they choose to go into, and that there'll be no need of their doing much only to let things grow. The real estate agents encourage that notion. They're the gol-darndest lot I ever saw. They can't talk reasonable, and they never quit their everlasting blowing. You'd think they were fairly crazy about this country. It will almost make a man who knows the situation vomit the way they talk. Murderation, they've got dodges to beat any Eastern man that ever lived. They always like to take a possible customer to ride to show him around. Crowd him into your rig some way, and then your sale is half made. Otherwise, a rival will take the drive with him and your chance in that quarter is gone. It isn't the habit to exhibit any anxiety to sell. You point out this and that piece of property and talk about what it is suited for and what its future value will probably be, and you're pretty sure to get your man interested.

"Everybody deals in real estate, ministers and all. Some of the ministers get so tangled up they have to leave their pulpits. You have no idee of the state of things. I know one Methodist minister who has done particularly well. When he notices a new man in his congregation he of course takes pains to shake hands and welcome him, and then he asks if he is going to settle. If the man says, 'Yes,' the minister mentions that while he is not in the real estate business he knows of various pieces of property for sale and would be glad to render any assistance he could. You see, the members of his flock place whatever piece of land they want to dispose of in his hands, and he lists it and sells it on a per cent the same as any other agent. But he is supposed by the purchaser to be disinterested, and he talks with the stranger's family, holds prayers with them and keeps them right under his thumb. You can't never persuade the preacher's man away. He's got a dead sure thing, and by and by the sale is made and the rest of us say, 'The parson has landed another man all right.'

"Then there's a kind of agent who has no office or no nothing. He keeps watch of the streets. When he sees strangers standing around in the sun trying to get warm he happens up to 'em and says, 'Kind o' cold this morning.'

"That leads to talk, and if he finds they have some notion of buying property he says, 'Well, I ain't got no property to sell, myself, but there's a friend of mine has just about what you're lookin' for, and I'd be glad to take you around to see it.'

"Darned if he ain't about the best man in town, next to the preacher, to make sales! The strangers perhaps wouldn't go in the door of a real estate office, but they buy of him because they think he has no money interest in making the sale. They may even brag afterward to the real estate men who have offices, and say, 'We bought through him because we didn't want to pay you fellers a commission.'

"Another way to force sales is to employ what they call a 'striker.' Suppose you are trying to sell a ranch. The striker comes in while you are talking with your customer, and you greet him as a person who owns a ranch close by the one you have for sale. You ask him what he'll take for his place, but he won't sell.

It's too profitable a property, while all the time the striker hasn't any place at all. One agent in the city I lived in was working to dispose of a tract of land to two ladies, and he represented it would have a very ready sale cut up for house lots, though it was miles beyond where the city was at all built up, and the city wouldn't grow to it in five hundred years. To speak the exact truth, it wa'n't worth a cuss. But he tells 'em

there's three or four parties after it who are liable to take it any time, and they'd better not delay. So they got the refusal of it for a few days. Before the time was up a striker called on 'em. He'd never shaved and had whiskers all around his face a foot long. You might say he was from Missouri. He was an old innocent-lookin' feller and made out he was deacon of some church, and he says, 'I understand you've bought that property, and I wanted to know about getting a part of it. I'm willing to give so much for half of it,' and he named a price bigger'n they were goin' to pay for the whole.

"They were all in a flutter, and they said that arrangements were not quite complete, but the property was about to be put on the market by them and he should have first chance. Then they made haste to buy and were the most tickled women in the world, but the man with the whiskers never came again. That old freak would land every victim he got hold of and take their last dollar. I was sorry for those women, but women do make the awfullest breaks in these land trades. They go into speculation head over heels.

"One day a stranger called at my office and told me he'd been in town two weeks and invested five thousand dollars. The tales of the land agents had made him enthusiastic, and he said, 'You people out here are slow. You stand around doing nothing and let us Eastern people make all the money.'

"He was sure he was going to double on his investment within a year, but he was soon ready to sell out at a heavy loss. There's no use talking—you pick up any property we had and it would pretty near burn your fingers. That's what it would. But new people were coming in on every train looking for property to invest in, and the papers were praising it up all the time, so that hearing of prices constantly on the rise they'd get in a hurry to buy. But a month was a long time for a place to be out of the market. By then a man was pretty sure to be sick of his bargain. When I made a sale I just checked it with a pencil. I didn't cross off the item for I'd soon have had my book scratched up and spoiled. In a few weeks, the property was bound to go on sale again, and then I'd simply erase the check. You could readily tell when a piece of property had recently changed hands, for there would be some little improvements made on it. That's the only time a man ever had any heart for laying out money and effort on his place.

"The other agents in town got onto me right straddle of my neck for not booming the region more, but I couldn't do it. If a man came to me and I found he had a family of children, I would urge him to keep his money and go back where he came from. If he was a single man, or there was only him and his wife, I showed what there was to be had and let him use his own judgment. But, by gosh, I didn't feel right even about that, and now I'm quit of the business."

Notes:

Los Angeles, the metropolis of Southern California, is naturally the first stopping-place of every tourist who arrives by the Santa Fe or Southern Pacific. In 1880 this "Town of the Queen of the Angels," as the Spaniards called it, had only eleven thousand inhabitants, but twenty-five years later there were nearly two hundred thousand. It is a modern big city, yet with environs that are peculiarly charming. Here is some of the finest fruit country on the west coast and you find innumerable groves of both orange and lemon trees, and the homes nestle among blossoms and green foliage even in midwinter. Then there is a background of rugged mountain heights, and not far away in the other direction is the sea and the enchanting island of Santa Catalina, reputed to be the greatest fishing-place on earth. Every facility is provided for seeing the towns and villages of the Los Angeles region and for climbing the mountains or going to the wild isle off the coast.

The most famous suburb of Los Angeles is

Pasadena. This, too, is a city, but for the most part is a place of homes, each with a setting of velvety turf and full-foliaged trees and flowers. It is a playground of wealth, the winter dwelling-place of a multitude of Eastern people and contains some of the finest residence thoroughfares on this continent. Various other flourishing towns and much of the best cultivated portion of this "Land of the Afternoon" can be glimpsed by taking a day's trip on a railway that makes a long loop back into the interior. Of the towns on this loop that would best repay a special visit, I think Riverside and Redlands should have the preference.

The country is least attractive in the parched months of the late summer and early autumn, and is seen at its best in April and May. As compared with the temperature that most of the states east of the Rocky Mountains experience in the colder months, the West Coast climate will be found very genial, but warm clothing, light overcoats, shawls, or convenient wraps which may be used or discarded according to one's needs, are an essential part of the traveller's outfit. The evenings and nights are sure to be cool, and chilling rains are a frequent feature of the winter.

SANTA BARBARA AND ITS HISTORIC MISSION

There had been rain early in the day, but as my train went northward from Los Angeles, the clouds rolled away, and when we came to the seashore the sun was shining from the west in a broad dazzling path of light across the restless waves. Off in the distance were some islands nearly hidden in silvery haze. A series of fine big hills hugged the ocean, and we skirted their bases close to the beach till we reached Santa Barbara where the hills gave place to a wide valley and disclosed a noble range of mountains rising along the east.

The lower portion of the town is a straggling and promiscuous set of buildings, and misses little of being squalid; but as you go farther back, homes of the suburban type become more and more numerous till you find nothing else but handsome cottages and villas hiding amid the semi-tropical luxuriance of blossoms and shrubbery. On a gentle hill at the end of the vale stands the Mission charming the beholder with its simplicity, its size, its imposing situation and its storied age. It is a structure that seems to belong to another realm and another civilization, and the only local buildings at all akin to it are a few lowly adobe houses in the town center, just off the main business street—survivals of the old Spanish village. These are usually whitewashed, and they have broad, tile-floored verandahs with roses, morning-glories or other vines growing along the front. Neither the chill of winter, nor the heat of summer can very well penetrate their massive earthen walls. As one of the dwellers said to me, "It might be August, and the sun no matter how hot, you go in this house, it be cold, nice, good."

He showed me a patch of grapevines

trimmed back to the bare stubs, but the green new sprouts were already well started, and he said, "They will have on them fine grapes—good to eat, good to make wine, and the wine is more strong as whiskey. See how these vines is growing. I have all the time to cut them back. He grow fast, queek! You bet you! By gosh, give him a chance and he grow all over the place! That is cactus over there. Prickly pear, I call him. The fruit has many pins on it—what you call them?—thorns. But get them off and the skin off, and the inside is sweet, good."

I asked him the name of a little flowering plant growing underfoot, but he only knew that it was a weed which was sometimes used for medicine. "It will keep you well better than the doctor," he continued. "If I be made sick of the stomach I boil it for a drink. Ah! the doctor cannot tell what is the trouble inside of you. He get him your money. He don't care whether you die."

I went into one old adobe. It was pretty dismal and dark and bare, and the rafters and roof-boards overhead were black with soot. The two things that most impressed me were the presence of a piano, and a sign hung on the wall that had been painted by some genius of the family and which said, 'Don't Spick in the Table'. The idea of the motto was not to chatter while eating.

In my wanderings about the old part of the town, I came across an Irishman converting a wayside blue gum that he had felled into firewood. The chopper was elderly, tattered and rusty, but in independent circumstances nevertheless, for he pointed across the road and affirmed that he owned an entire block of land

and the various cabins on it, property worth in his say-so fifteen or twenty thousand dollars. He mentioned that he lived over there, and I asked him in which house. He responded that he didn't live in any house but camped in a wagon which was hidden from view by some intervening buildings.

"Have ye been up to the ould Mission?" he queried, settling himself comfortably on the blue gum log. "It is an intheresting place to look about, and soom like to go to church there on Sundays. I wint wunst mesilf. A lady who thought a heap of me had invited me to go wid her, and she sat in the front seat. But I stayed near the door, and close by me was a lobby hole or box like a little room built ag'in the wall and I could hear a priest a-muttering in it. Yes, he was in there a-gobbling away like an ould turkey—joost as if the outside wasn't good enough for him and he moost go in there and gobble by himself, and I couldn't understand a word he said, for he didn't speak out plain and brave.

"There was a lot o' prayin' to be did in the church service, and you had to be crossin' yoursilf and pokin' your heart most of the time. But I wasn't coom for that. I was there to listen and look. I couldn't make mooch sinse out of what I heard because a good deal was in Latin or soom other haythen language. Then there was a feller walkin' around swingin' a thing that smoked—a cincer, they call it, and he was shakin' it this way and that and payin' no sort of attintion to it, and I said to mesilf, 'That feller is no Catholic. He don't care what he's got there, whether it's wather or a kag of beer or what it is.'

"I want ye to notice one place at the Mission particular. Turn off the road that goes up the hill joost beyond the main building and ye will see the ruins of three rooms. It's telled me that the ould monks walled some bad people in there to stay for the rest of their lives. The back most room was very small and half under the hill, and the opening into it was only a round hole that you had to crawl through on your face and hands. It seems like that was the place for thim that was very bad—the outlawed criminals. The others stayed in the bigger rooms where it was more plisant.

"But whin Fremont coom here he throwed a cannon ball or two at thim rooms, and he let the prisoners loose. He knowed what was there. I niver had thought well of his outfit coomin' here and raising thunder with the Spanish people, but whin I seen what he done in leaving those prisoners loose, I felt different. A man in this town who was in Fremont's army tould me about it, but he has been dead now a matther of five or six years. Ah! the ould padres had been havin' their own way till Fremont coom. They got all the Indians workin' for 'em and were bossin' thim and makin' thim do exactly as they pleased and tellin' thim if they didn't obey they'd be sint to hell sure. So the padres got so rich and proud they didn't hardly want to speak to anyone. Thim prison rooms make a strange-lookin' ruin even yit, and the firrust time I was past the hair fairly stood up on me head at the sight. I thought I would as soon have me coffin made and be put in the ground as be walled in there."

Really, the buildings of which he spoke had something to do with the storage and filtering of the

old water supply, and there never was any such grim prison as he described. The Mission itself, unlike most of the California Missions, is not a ruin, but is in excellent repair and still the dwelling of the gowned and sandaled monks, as it was a century ago. These monks are so different from ordinary folk in their garments and in the strangely decorative life they lead that it is fascinating to watch them engaged in their various duties. The furniture and all the belongings of the Mission are severely simple, but the great court back of the main building is full of flowers and trees, and its luxuriance contrasts oddly with the severity of the interiors. Throngs of visitors are constantly coming and going. They, however, only have access to certain public portions of the premises, so that those portions where the friars eat and sleep and do their daily tasks in shops and garden and fields repose in almost unbroken calm.

From the Mission, I went far up a mountain roadway that for a long distance clung to a hillside well up above a noisy stream coursing along in the wooded hollow. The road was muddy and gullied. Heavy wagons were going up after stone, or returning loaded, and there were many equestrians—ladies, men and children. Santa Barbara is a famous place for horseback expeditions. Nearly everyone rides, even those who before they go there never have been on a horse, and all through the day you see the riders, singly, in couples and in squads, gallivanting through the town streets, and meet them on every road and trail for miles around.

The road I was on was bordered by pastures that in places were grassy but were largely covered with gray-green sagebrush mingled with thickets of chaparral misted over at that season with blue blossoms. In favored spots grew the cactus and clumps of great century plants. When there was open grazing land, it was strewn with rocks, and this rocky ground seemed to favor the growth of scattered groves of live oaks. The oaks were wonderfully twisted and distorted, their bark was gray with lichen and they looked as ancient as the rock-strewn hills on which they stood.

At one point, I came on a herd of cattle feeding along the brushy roadside, and three boys were watching them. The watchers were playing with a pet cow that was lying down and that seemed to take a sort of sleepy pleasure in their proceedings. The clothing of the lads was covered with dirt and hairs, for they tumbled about on the ground or leaned on the creature and rubbed it companionably. One boy was milking into his mouth. The oldest of the trio said, "My father gave me this cow when she was a little bit of a calf, and I take care of her. If he tries to milk her he gets kicked, but I can milk her anywhere. Last December she pretty near died. There was no feed in the pastures, and the cattle was dying all over. We lost quite a few, and this cow got so weak she would tumble down. So we carried feed to her and she got stronger. We watch the cattle here all day but at noontime take turns going home to dinner. When night comes, we drive the cattle into the pasture.

I went on until the foothills began to merge into the rough steeps of the mountains, and then I wandered back to the town.

On my last afternoon in Santa Barbara I again had a talk with the Irishman-of-wealth who lived in a wagon. He was still laboring at the big blue gum, but desisted from his exertion to sit down and chat, as readily as he had before. He was especially eager to know what I thought of the Mission and its monks and their religion. Soon he was relating some of his personal opinions and experiences.

"I'm not mooch stuck on religion mesilf," said he, and a little church-going lasts me a long time. Wunst my fri'nds tould me I ought to go to confession. So I said I would, and at the church where they tuk me I wint into a little room, and there was two chairs and a priest, and he and me set down. Thin he began moombling along like a drunken man wid a pipe in his mouth. Well, I listened and listened, and as I could make no sinse at all out of his moombling, I said nothing. At last he got up and says, 'Adieu, coom again,' and I says, 'All right,' and wint out.

"Last week a Salvationist preacher was along the road here, and he stopped to speak wid me as I was hackin' away at this tree. He wanted me to go to church. I tould him I wouldn't care if there was niver a church in the world. 'I don't believe in your Bible,' I says. 'There's good things in it, but there's the divil and everything else besides in it, and it tells lies the same as the rest of the people.'

'Brother,' he says, 'ye moostn't think that way.'

" 'Well,' I says, 'you take sooch a story as that about Noah and how God raised the wather of the Pacific Ocean and turned it topsided like over Asia and drowned all the people—I can't bel'ave it. Would God be that cruel?'

" 'He was not cruel,' the Salvationist said. 'There was an ark, and whin the flood came and the people was all a-swimming, God tould thim to come into the ark, and they would not.'

" 'How could they all get in?' I says. 'It wouldn't have held thim.'

"Eh-heh!' he kind o' stammered, 'God can do

anything. He made the world.'

" 'What did he make it out of?' I asked.

"He made it out of doost,' says the Salvationist.

"And who made the doost?' I says.

"Ha-ha-ha-ha-ha! I ketched him there, and he got mad at me. 'You can get soom kids to believe thim things,' I says, 'but it's no use to be arguin' to a sinsible, intilligent man. I keep the straight thrack and I want no more of this nonsinsical talk.' "

The chopper took his hat off and ran his fingers thoughtfully through his hair. Then he resumed his remarks by asking, "Did ye iver know there was gold in Ireland? Well, whin I was a kid I lived about twinty miles from the city of Cork, and near me home was a nice creek—not like these streams in California, but clear and beautiful and running all the time; and wan day I see a bright stone in the wather—it might be about the size of a goose's egg, and I picked it up. I had niver seen anything like it—so yaller and heavy, and it took me eye. So I carried it home to me mother and she put it under the bed.

"Me mother had been nurse in a gintleman's family, a family that was way up, and the gintleman's daughter would soomtimes coom and call on her. The young lady was there wan time all dhressed up so very fine, and me mother showed her the yaller stone from under the bed, and the young lady carried it away wid her.

"I didn't know what the stone was thin, but since I been in this country and worked in the mines I know it was a lump of pure gold. I seen in that creek other stones like it, and going right across the creek was a vein of what I called white rocks, that now I would call honeycomb quartz-gold bearing. If I broke the rock, the pieces would hang together wid the gold in it. Soomtimes I would pick up one o' the gold pebbles, and it seemed so heavy I would toss it up joost to feel it coom down chuck in the palm of me hand. If it fell on the ground it would make the doost fly, it was that heavy. Ah, there's plinty of rich ore in Ireland, and what's the matther they don't give the people per-mission for to mine it? I s'pose if I was to go back there and try to get that gold they'd put me in jail, eh?

"Well, now, I was by the creek another time where there was a deep hole wid a ruffle below it, and in this deep place I see soom throut. Wan was ahead and the others was following like a lot of dogs running after another, goin' along in rotation. The first throut had soomthing in its mouth—oh, so shining—joost like sunlight. Pretty soon the throut dropped it, and the next one picked it up and the rest kept on chasing until he dropped it and another ketched it, and away wid it. Ha-ha-ha-ha-ha! I kept watchin' and by and by I got hold o' the shining thing—and what was it but a di'mond. I didn't know thin, though, what it was, and I ran home and showed it to me mother and said, 'Oh, look what a nice little rock I got!'

But she let the gintleman's daughter take it, and the young lady put it in a ring. I worked at her house whin I got older, and she would show me the ring wid the di'mond in it and make it flash the light over on the wall, and she would tell how she had the value of so mooch wealth on her finger. That's the way people have cheated me all me life—because I would niver grab for anything.

"Perhaps not iveryone would have seen what I seen. Soom of us are odd from the balance of the people. I have tould you about the gold and the di'mond, but the most wonderful thing in me life is that I have seen the fairies. Me father seen 'em too, and he said his father did before him, and so I suppose have all the ginerations in our family from the commincement of the world right down. I remimber the first time I seen 'em I was a boy out in the pasture. I was all alone, and I seen forty or fifty little men goin' along, and they were no more than three feet high. They wore stove-pipe hats and bobtail coats and knee-breeches, and each had a big long pipe in his mouth, and they stood up so straight and plump and nice it was a pleasure to look at 'em. Ye see they was dhressed in the rael ould-time Irish costume. I have seen the Scotch costume and the other national costumes, and soom are good enough, and soom are crazy-like, but none are equal to the Irish. I tell you an Irishman in that ould dhress looked like a smart, intilligent, brave man. Ivery wan o' those fairy men carried a blackthorn stick. Ah, how mooch the ould Irish did think o' their blackthorns! How they did bile 'em in hot wather and rub thim wid ile, and hang thim up in the chimney to get seasoned and smoked, and they always carried thim to protict thimsilves when they wint to a fair.

"Well, there was a bird in Ireland used to coom and sing to me a little black bird like wan o' these pewees. Whin I took shipping for this counthry I felt very bad to be leavin' me little bird. I said, 'Oh, I'm so sorry! I'm afraid I shall lose me luck.'

"But after we was about ten days out I looked back, and there I saw me little pewee coomin', and he flew like he was awful tired. Finally, he caught up wid us and lit on the topmast, and there he stayed the rest of the day. The next morning, he was down on the first yard, and the day after that he was on the bulwarks. I was on the promenade poop forward, and I spoke to him, and he coom and hopped about and e't soom of a piece of bread I had, and then he hollered, 'Pe-wee-wee-wee-wee!' and flew back up in the riggin'.

"After a while I wint down below, and whin I coom up again I couldn't see him at all any more. But he visits me lots o' times since I been in this counthry. It's the same bird, wid the same motions and song my little bird in Ireland had. I could tell him from any other bird. He cooms and gives me warnin' if soomthin' is goin' to go bad. Maybe now and then, he will appear as a cow. There was wunst I had a little bit of a log cabin down the coast a few miles, and there was a good stout fince around it, and barley a-growin' in the yard. Well, I was settin' in me cabin wan day whin a cow stuck her head in the door and laughed joost like a Christian. 'How did you get inside my fince?' I said. 'It's destroyin' my barley, ye are.'

"So I drove her out of the gate, and I was astonished she wint so quick and peaceable, and not ugly and conniptious like most cows. Thin I looked at the barley, but it was not hurt at all. Another day I found the cow rubbin' herself against the side of my little house, and I drove her off across the fields till she passed around soom bushes, and the next minute she coom in sight and a calf wid her. She passed behind soom more bushes, and as soon as she appeared again there was half dozen more cows wid her. Ha-ha-ha-ha! I picked up a rock to throw at her, but she looked me such a look I did not throw. 'That's the ould fairies,' I said, and I asked forgiveness.

"The cow kept foolin' wid me for about a month. I wa'n't feelin' well, and I was gettin' worse. 'Oh,' I thought, 'I'm goin' to die!'

"I took a walk out wan day, and I seen that cow by the side of the road, and I stopped and had a good look at her. 'What a fine cow!' I says, 'and how full your bag is wid milk! I niver noticed that before. I will bring a bucket and milk you and have soom bread and milk to eat.'

"So I got the bucket and kneeled down to milk, but the cow began to hitch around and would not stand still, and I said, 'If you don't quit that I'll hit you wid the bucket.'

"She lifted up wan hind foot like she was goin' to kick, and she turned her head around and looked at me as if she was human and had sinse. I was scared and I started to escape into a near field. Well, now thin, as I was goin' over the fince I looked back and there was no cow to be seen. She'd gone out of sight while I was takin' three steps.

"The next evening I was out again, and there was the cow in the road, and the milk was runnin' out of her bag and down the road in a regular stream to the gulch. I hurried and brought me bucket and caught about two inches in the bottom of it. Thin I carried it to the house and had soom bread and milk, and that milk was delicious, palatable, fine. It was the best I iver tasted. It made another man of me. I could feel the change at wunst. It braced me up and I was well.

"I had soom milk left and I thought I would let it stay in the bucket and have it in the morning, but when morning came and I looked in the bucket I saw nothing but wather there. At noon I looked in again. and the bucket was dry. Now, what do you call that? It was the fairies all the same havin' fun wid me. I was sick and they cured me. They knowed it was no bother to do it.

"The fairies had a hand too in my gettin' this block of land I own. They showed me the picture of it before I left Ireland, and the minute I set eyes on it I was certain it was what they intinded I should have. Thin, wan time here, the fairies tould me I could have great herds of cattle or sheep or pigs. 'Whativer kind of animals ye want ye can have,' they said, and I chose the cattle, and no sooner did I say the word than up coom a band of cattle out of the ground—hoondreds av thim. 'There they are,' the fairies said, 'and in twinty years thim will be yours, and the ranch they're on, if ye want thim.'

"Well, they were on a ranch where a lady named Hale lived, and ivery cow had two calves a year, and things wint along very prosperous. The fairies was workin' on the lady, too, and she had her eye on me, and she knew me fairy cows was on her ranch, and that I was joost givin' up to her the twinty years' use av thim. So whin the time was gone, she cooms and wants me to marry her, but I thought I'd go along on me own hook. Oh, this is a very peculiar sort of a woruld—this is!"

My comrade rose and chopped a few strokes, but the day was drawing to an end. Some fellow-laborers passed on the street and shouted a greeting to him and he concluded to stop work. He put on his vest and coat, took up his axe and saw and started for home. I went with him, and we walked around into the lot where, back of a neighbor's shed, he had his queer habitation. It was a big old lumber wagon with a piece of canvas spread from the high seat down toward the back. The shelter afforded was poor and cramped. A few other belongings were scattered about in the grass and there was a wreck of a stove that could still be made to serve after a fashion. But then, though to me these household effects seemed meagre and shabby, I do not know that they so impressed the owner. He had the gift of imagination, and beautiful as is nature in that region, and delightful as is the ancient Mission, there is nothing in my visit I remember with more pleasure than this man with his visions of realms beyond my ken.

Notes:

Santa Barbara is one of the most attractive towns in California, beautiful in its surrounding scenery, not so large as to be dominated by commercialism, nor so small as to be rude and lacking in comfortable accommodations. The old survives amid the new, and you can even yet find buildings and life that have the characteristics of the time of Spanish rule. Here is the best preserved of all the old Missions. Every Mission is worth seeing, but Santa Barbara has one where the gowned and sandaled monks still dwell and labor.

The chief outdoor pleasures for the sojourner here are coaching, cross-country horseback riding, fishing, and hunting. Most visitors would be interested to read the account of early days in Santa Barbara to be found in Dana's *Two Years Before the Mast*. This book, in fact, entertainingly describes the aspect and customs of every old sea town from San Francisco to San Diego.

The climate in this region is mild and equable, but it is also excessively dry, with the result that the roads are dusty most of the year. In the winter and spring, however, during the rainy season, they are often so heavy as to be impassable for automobiles in the mountain sections. But, as a rule, the coast roads out of Santa Barbara are fairly good, though there are always some dubious spots. The main motor route continues south to Los Angeles and San Diego, and north to San Francisco.

A VALE OF PLENTY

California has a number of valleys that are at the same time remarkable for their great size and their productive capacity, but the San Joaquin excels any of the others. A few decades ago it was not esteemed of much use except for grazing, though certain parts would grow excellent crops of wheat, but irrigation has changed all this, and as you pass through it on the train you marvel at the seemingly endless succession of thriving fields and orchards.

My first day in the valley was a Sunday spent at a little village consisting mostly of a hotel and a few stores and saloons facing the railway. Round about was a vast level extending for miles in every direction, and nearly all of it green with wheat. At long intervals, amid this green sea could be discerned a small huddle of buildings where there was a ranch house. It was one of the regions in which, when the grain ripens, a harvester is used that is drawn by thirty-six mules or horses, and that cuts off the heads of the wheat, threshes out the grain and drops it in sacks behind. Forty acres will be covered daily on good ground and the season lasts three months. After the harvester has finished, the cattle are turned onto the land and they feed on the stubble and trample it so it can be ploughed under.

For an hour or two in the morning I sat on the hotel piazza a little way from a group of men gathered near the door of the odorous barroom. The day was quiet and warm. The flies buzzed, and some sparrows chattered noisily and flitted about with bits of straw and bark and string for their nest-building beneath the cornice of the piazza. A few teams were hitched to railings under the umbrella trees along the sidewalk, and there were occasional passers on the highway. One

of these passers was a man driving two burros laden with packs. The creatures walked slowly and patiently and he followed behind. He was from some mine, and all his outfit and belongings were on the donkeys. A boy on horseback rode up in front of the hotel and borrowed the proprietor's gun that he might do a little hunting. A tramp came along and wanted something to eat, and he was set at work chopping wood. Except for him it was a day of loafing and recreation.

The largest group of loiterers gathered in front of the post office to watch or participate in a game of marbles. The players were young men and boys. A little fellow named Danny was getting the advantage when I joined the on-lookers, and a young man in blue trousers, who was addressed as "Chub," was about to snap his taw at Danny's. "I want to kill Danny," he said, "and make him give up his winnings."

But he missed, and his marble rolled under the piazza. "Well, I'll be dog-goned!" he exclaimed. "That's just the way my luck runs today."

The piazza underpinning was boarded nearly to the ground. He lay down and reached unsuccessfully into the gloom. Then several others tried it, and at last one of them got a stick to poke with, and pretty soon secured the taw.

"It's Al's shot, ain't it?" asked Danny.

"Look out for me. I'm comin'!" cried Al.

To his disgust his taw stopped in the ring, and the rules obliged him to drop in a marble to get it out. "Well, that fattens the ring, anyhow," he said philosophically as he made the exchange. "Knock down there, Nick, it's your turn."

Nick's taw was near the ring, and that he might make a sure shot he punched up a little heap of dirt where a marble lay in the ring and put the marble on top. His method proved a success, and Chub said, "He sets the marble up on a nubbin and then fudges it right off. Us fellers had better holler when he gets ready again so he won't shoot straight. That's what the boys used to do at school. It always mixed me up and made me mad, and I'd fight. But it didn't do no good if I did fight. I'd get licked every time."

Nick made careful preparations for a second shot, but just as he snapped his taw his comrades all shouted, and he was so confused he missed. The taw rolled along and hit someone's foot. "Kicks on!" the players cried, and the one who had stopped it gave it a poke with his foot to carry it where he thought it would naturally have gone.

"You're havin' a pretty hot game," commented a newcomer.

"It's a warm one, I tell yer," responded Al.

"I was afraid this was goin' to be a lonesome old day," said Chub, "but I've had a lot of fun," and the game continued hour after hour until dinner time. Then the participants divided the marbles, for they did not play for keeps, and went their several ways.

The Sabbath as I saw it here is characteristic of the Far West. Nearly everywhere it is a holiday to a very marked extent, and church-going is decidedly less the habit than in the East. Ball games are one of the most popular of the amusements of the day, and when I chanced to spend a Sabbath at Visalia, a busy town in the heart of one of the best portions of the valley, the chief event of the day was the getting out of the fire engine for a little sport and practice squirting around the streets.

It was the rainy season, and we had several heavy downpours that night which left the region pretty thoroughly soaked. However, the sun shone forth the next morning, and in spite of the miry walking I started for a long ramble among the farms. I had to do a good deal of dodging to get around the pools and puddles, and there were certain of the "slues" in the hollows which almost brought me to a stop. Yet by climbing along on fences or resorting to the embankment of an irrigating ditch, or by cutting across a field I contrived to continue my ramble.

The country was good to look at in spite of the over-abundance of mud and water. On the eastern horizon rose ranges of snowy mountains, but the lowlands were a green paradise. The grazing fields, in particular, were very beautiful with their cattle, horses, or hogs, and with their scattering ancient oaks. These oaks abounded but never gathered in a thick wood. They were wide-spreading and stately and made the country look like a park. Other native trees were very few, except along the streams, which were apt to be thickly screened by willows and cottonwoods. Many great tracts of land were set out to regular rows of prune and peach trees, and every farmhouse seemed to have its packing shed and its great heap of wooden drying-trays. Formerly pears were a staple fruit, but some sort of a blight has put the trees out of business.

The people I met and spoke with were agreed that it was an unusual condition to have too much water, and the owners of the flooded lands were not altogether happy, yet any damage they suffered was largely offset by the drowning of such pests as the gophers and ground squirrels. The local conditions therefore were on the whole satisfactory, but certain other sections had not fared so well. For instance, in the same county, there used to be a lake thirty miles broad and a hundred long. It afforded fine fishing, and the hunters resorted to it to shoot the abounding ducks and geese. Gradually it dried away and left some of the richest farmland in the world. The old lake-bed became a great wheat-producing district, but now the heavy rains had begun to fill the basin of the former lake, and the body of water was fast expanding to its former size. The wheat had grown to be waist high and was well headed out, but the lake-bed dwellers had to abandon everything except the little they could carry away, and, driving their stock before them, they sought more elevated ground. It was thought that many years must pass before the water would again dry away.

As I walked on I at length wandered into a little village. Near its center I stopped on the piazza of a bakeshop. Here was a chair, a settee and several boxes occupied by a row of men smoking, spitting and talking. The weather was not propitious for field work, and the piazza group was in a very leisurely and hospitable frame of mind. If anyone passed, either walking or driving, they never failed to shout out an invitation to stop. "Come and join us," they would say. "You'll never find a better lookin' crowd in your life."

If the passer was riding, the remarks would continue, "Aw! get out and tie up. Take a rest. Don't be in such a rush."

Presently a fellow approached driving a smart span of horses attached to a gig. "Hold on to them ribbons thar!" was the cry from the piazza.

The man in the gig slowed down and halted. His vehicle was old and weatherbeaten, but it had a bright red whiffletree. "Why didn't you paint the rest of your gig?" someone queried.

"Well," said the driver, "I left it that way so people'd ask questions."

"Say, but you would shine if your gig was all painted that style," remarked one of the lookers-on.

"This is a nice little team," said the occupant of the gig. "I've driven 'em about fifteen miles and now I think I'll put 'em in the stable."

"Oh, no, don't do that," said someone on the porch. "Drive 'em some more. It'll make 'em eat their hay good."

Shortly after he had gone a man in a top buggy drove up in front of the bakeshop, and one of the loafers said, "Looks like you was goin' somewhere."

The man in the buggy poked his head out and said, "Who wants to go to town with me and get drunk?" Some responded that they would like well enough to get drunk, but none of them cared to exert themselves sufficiently to go to town, and he had to continue his journey alone.

The man of the piazza gathering who interested me most was an old settler of the region who had come from Tennessee in 1870. "But the country had been occupied some for nearly twenty years before that," he observed. "In 1852 there was eight or ten families built a stockade at Visalia and then put up their log cabins against it around on the outside. The Indians was dangerous, you see, and even after I come, the danger wa'n't past. They'd kill our cattle, and they'd take your scalp if they had a good chance.

"This country in its natural state was a forest of oak with here and there an open where the tall grass grew. We used to cut the grass for hay. Land could be had almost for the asking. You only needed to take up a homestead right from the government, and when you had paid sixteen dollars and lived on the land five years you were owner of a quarter section—one hundred and sixty acres. Deer, antelopes and wild mustangs was plenty. You'd often see the antelopes feeding in among the cattle. People e't their meat, but it was coarse and not so good as deer meat. You could go up there in those foothills you see to the east and kill a wagon load of deer in a day. They roamed about fifty to a hundred in a band.

"Bears was common up in the mountains—brown, cinnamon, black and grizzlies—but I wa'n't lookin' for them fellers. I was willin' to make friends. If they'd let me alone I'd let them alone, you bet yer boots I would. But one time I was up there helpin' old Billy Rhoades with his sheep. Fred Stacy was with me, and we was goin' across a little medder when we see a full-grown grizzly bear with a cub follerin' her, and they was comin' straight toward us.

"It happened there was a cluster of smallish pine trees nearby, and Fred went up one tree and I went up another. I didn't have a thing to shoot with, and I don't suppose I'd have used a gun if I'd had one. The bear kind o' looked up at us but kept on down the trail. She found our camp, and she turned over our potatoes and beans and scattered them and our other things all about. Yes, she had a regular tear-up. But I was glad to git off with no worse damage. A bear with a cub will fight, you know, and I come as clost to a grizzly then as I want to, less'n the bear was in a cage.

"Another time old man Rhoades and his son was fetchin' some sheep off the mountains, and the boy went into a canyon for a drink. He lay down to git at the water when a black bear jumped out of the willers onto him and begun a-chawin' him. He hollered for the old man, who come hurryin' down—and there was the bear chawin' on his boy. The only thing the old man had to attack the bear with was a pocket knife. That was a poor weapon, but he saw he had the job to do, and he didn't hesitate. The bear was on the boy, and the old man was on the bear, and he got her, and he skinned her afterward. She mighty nigh killed the boy, and the old man was so tore and scratched he carried the scars to his grave.

"Anyone could have a horse in the early days by just goin' out and ketchin' a wild mustang. The way we used to do that was to build a corral consisting of a fence about eight feet high around a half acre or so, with a long wing fence extending out from it. Then when we see some mustangs feeding near we'd go out on the far side of 'em and give a yell to start 'em, and by heading 'em off we'd drive 'em against the wing fence and run 'em right into the corral. After that a man would go in and lasso one. He'd have to be on horseback or they'd run right over him.

"When he got a mustang roped he'd drag him out, put on a bridle and saddle, blindfold him and get on. The mustang didn't like that, and he'd begin to buck. Seems to me I've seen 'em buck as high as that schoolhouse over across the road. No matter what the mustang did, the rider had got to stick on. That was the only way those horses could be broke. They were the meanest things you ever see. They were good saddle ponies though—fine! An ordinary horse wouldn't stand half what they would. The mustangs were small, but they were tough and hardy—kind o' like a Jack rabbit. You could run one all day, and it would be about as good at the end as when it started, and the next morning it would buck off if you wa'n't careful.

"When I come here, cattle, sheep and hogs were all the go. There was very little soil cultivated, but gradually it got to be a great wheat country. Now wheat has given way to orchards, and we ship fruit all over the world. Alfalfa is grown quite a little and is more of a money-maker than fruit. It's ready to cut now, and we're only waiting till the weather is settled so we can cure it. We git four or five crops by the time the frosts bring the season to an end. It's good feed for cattle and all right for horses if you use some grain hay with it. By grain hay I mean barley and wheat cut when it is in a stiff dough—that is with the grain just past the milk stage.

"I used to raise wheat, but we had fifteen dry seasons right a-running which did me up. Now the weather seems to have changed and I look for fifteen wet seasons. So I'm goin' to try wheat again. You ain't sure of a crop unless you irrigate. When we people come here from the East we didn't know anything about irrigation. But somebody tried it and found it a success. Then we all turned loose. It's a good thing. At the same time, there's a lot of hard, dirty work in irrigating.

"First you're obliged to plough and scrape till you've got your land level and in check. We put two or three acres in a check with a levee around it. The checks have to be smaller if the land is rough. Our land here is pretty smooth, and two men with a pair of horses can git a quarter section in order—leveling checks, making ditches and floodgates, all in about a couple of months. But you are out something right along digging to keep the channels clear and making repairs. Still, if a man would give me a place back in Tennessee whar I come from I wouldn't take it nohow, if I had to live on it. In a wet season your corn would turn yaller as a punkin—it was aggravatin'!

"To show you what can be done here I want to tel you about a little orchard of apricots I bought a year ago. Everybody claimed it was run out, but I trimmed the trees and worked the ground and I got eight tons of fruit which I sold for twenty dollars a ton. That was better than a thump on the head with a sharp stone, wa'n't it?

"You can raise anything that will grow on the top side of the earth, in this valley. I got only two objections to it—in over half the land there's alkali, and secondly malaria is a good deal too common. You notice our houses ain't got cellars and are set up on posts off the ground—some of 'em three or four feet. That's 's on account of malaria.

"Perhaps it strikes you the houses must be cold in winter, but we don't have such sharp weather as they have in other parts of United States. I ain't seen but one snowfall in all the time I been here. You take a person from back East and drop 'em down here in March and they think they're in Paradise. Thar's an old lady from Iowa just come lately to this place, and she it is the prettiest country she ever cast her eyes on. When she come everybody was freezin' and hoverin' over the fire in Iowa, while here it wa'n't cold worth mentioning, and she says, 'Here I'll live and here I'll die.'

"But things ain't always so pleasant in our valley as people think they're goin' to be. Thar's a mighty lot gits fooled. They think they can pick up twenty-dollar gold pieces, dog-gone-it, and they have it all figured out how easy they can make their fortunes. So as soon as they see a piece of property that they fancy they just dive in and pay a good round price. Then when they find they can't git rich in a few weeks like they expected, they're sorry they grabbed so quick. Often they're so homesick that they're ready to take whatever anybody'll give for the property they've bought. There's an old negro here has picked up a lot of land from such fellers till he's got fifteen or twenty sections, and it's all paid for, too. He's a mighty good one. What he agrees to do he does, and he's looked up to about as much as anyone in this region. He's a cattle-man and a hog-man and has money laid away. Every one of his girls that gets married he gives five thousand dollars and a piece of land. That's a pretty good starter, eh?

"The poor investments that are made by strangers are mostly the fault of the real estate agents. I know of a man who sold out in Kansas and come here and a real estate agent induced him to buy a section of old alkali land at forty dollars an acre—made him believe it was the richest land in the country. The agent done wrong. I call that robbery. The land wouldn't sprout backyard peas. It wa'n't fitten to look at. Even salt grass wouldn't grow on some of it. You know what poor stuff salt grass is. The cattle will eat it when they can't get anything else, but it's tough and they got to have good teeth to bite it, and it won't fatten 'em any. Well, that man put up a house and a barn and a corral before he found out what sort of a bargain he'd made. He finally went back to where he come from, and his buildings are standing empty. He's got his money in that place, and he'll never get it out.

"Of course a good many fellers have taken land and made money, but there's a blamed sight more who have lost."

As a whole, the region around Visalia looked productive and prosperous, and in order to see some of the poorer land of the valley, I went on farther north. It so happened that I reached the place I had selected soon after five in the morning. There was no station— only a half dozen little homes and two or three small dilapidated stores, and a white schoolhouse that stood by itself off a quarter of a mile on the open unfenced prairie. A streak of yellow above the serrated peaks of an endless chain of snowy mountains in the east gave promise of the dawn. On the telegraph lines perched a twittering group of linnets. Nearby was a box freight car, and while I stood looking around me, a tramp slid out of the car, shouldered his bag and went off along the track, but on the outskirts of the settlement he stopped, built a little fire, and I suppose cooked himself some sort of a breakfast.

I walked out on the prairie. Here and there I could see scattered houses—rather forlorn-looking places most of them, and usually with no thought whatever bestowed on appearances. The plain was perfectly treeless, except that an occasional home had about it a few shade or fruit trees, and now and then a cluster of willow bushes grew beside the irrigating ditches. The ditches conveyed water to some alfalfa farms two or three miles away where the soil was deeper. Most of the land in the neighborhood was only fit for grazing, and close under the surface lay "hardpan"—a soft sandstone. At one place I came across men at work setting out fruit trees. They were on low ground where the soil had accumulated a little, but in order that the tree roots might have a chance to develop satisfactorily, the workers were blasting holes in the hardpan, one for each tree. A few horses, cows and goats were staked out near the village homes, and I saw a drove of black hogs munching along over the knolls, and late in the forenoon a vast flock of sheep drifted past.

A squad of men from the nearest town were ploughing, scraping and grading the road, which heretofore had never been turnpiked. The soil was very hard, and one of the men said, "It's rough on the tools. I had a new plough yesterday and in three hours I wore the point plumb out. I don't see how these fellers that

keep store here make a livin'. They never seem to be doin' no outside work and there's mighty few customers. Most o' the time they stand at the door lookin' for us to come in and spend the money we make on the road. Yet they wear good clothes and smoke a cigarette once in a while. One of 'em has a sheep ranch. I guess he's gettin' along all right. He had a Jim Dandy little wagon come to him on the train last week."

The man now turned to his work and I went to watch some boys not far away who were gathered around a small pond grabbing for pollywogs. They said they were going to use them for fish bait, and they had started to tell me about their luck in fishing when the bell in the schoolhouse cupola gave a few jingles. At once the boys dropped the pollywogs and scudded away across the prairie to the temple of learning.

For the sake of variety, I went in to have a look at one of the stores. It was not much more than a shanty and the supply of goods was very meagre.

"Billy" McDonald was the proprietor. I found him a good deal disturbed because his horse was missing. "I left her loose in the stable last night," said he, "and she got out and has gone back to town where I bought her not long ago."

A customer came in. He was a stranger who happened to be driving through the place and he wanted to purchase some soap. Billy seemed surprised. He didn't carry such an article in his stock. "Neither did the other store," he explained. So the customer bought a glass of whiskey instead.

Later in the day I again took the train and was soon in a region more favored. Indeed, in my memory of the valley I see little else than a constant succession of orchards and vineyards and great wheat fields and luxuriant pastures. But the homes did not seem in keeping with nature's affluence. Many were unpainted, unshaded, shabby and small, and looked as if in the heat of summer, they would be blistered off the face of the earth. Few were such as we in our older Eastern states would consider at all attractive or comfortable. That the Vale of Plenty should have its imperfections is to be expected. On the other hand, its attractions are many, and there lies before it a future full of promise.

Notes:

The San Joaquin Valley is one of the great agricultural basins of the world. It is two hundred and fifty miles long by about fifty wide. In it grows half the wheat raised in the state, and wheat farms of ten thousand to fifty thousand acres are not uncommon Here, too, you may see thousands of acres of alfalfa, vast vineyards and astonishingly large orchards of prunes, peaches, apricots, figs and other fruits. It produces nearly all the raisins of the United States, and fabulous crops of asparagus, potatoes, beans and melons and it is famous for its cattle, sheep and hogs. Stop at any of the chief towns, such as Visalia, Fresno, or Stockton, and journey out into the surrounding country and see what is being done. Irrigation is the chief dependence for producing crops, and water for this purpose is abundant.

Another attraction of the valley is the excursions that can be made from it into the Sierras. Best of all is a visit to the Yosemite, but scarcely less interesting is a trip to the wild canyon of King's River. This latter journey is made from Visalia, partly by stage, partly by pack and saddle train. The gorge lacks the waterfalls of the Yosemite, and its walls are not so precipitous, but they rise into even wilder and more stupendous heights. On account of snow and flooded streams, July and August are the best months for the trip. To add to the fascination of this jaunt you have close at hand Mount Whitney, the loftiest mountain in the United States, if we except the Alaskan giants. It is easily ascended from the west side. The streams are full of trout, and game abounds. Still another attraction of the region is the General Grant National Park containing many of the famous big trees.

The Sierra Nevada (in English the words mean Snowy Range) sweeps along the eastern borders of California for fully five hundred miles. It abounds in scenery of marvellous grandeur, and offers many attractions to the Alpine explorer.

The Union Pacific Railroad, as it climbs the mountains toward Nevada, passes through thirty-seven miles of snowsheds.

Although Mount Whitney which soars up 14,502 feet is the highest point in the United States, it is a curious fact that only seventy-five miles away is the lowest point, two hundred and seventy-five feet below the sea-level, in Death Valley. This valley acquired its name from the loss of numerous emigrants who attempted to pass through it in 1849.

APRIL IN THE YOSEMITE

From the San Joaquin Valley, I went by a branch railroad to Raymond far back in the Sierra foothills. The journey was delightful. Everywhere were flowery fields and pastures, and at times the wastelands were fairly covered with radiant blossoms. Some of the patches and streaks of bloom were blue, some purple,

some white, and still others were a blaze of reds and yellows. The poppies were perhaps the most abundant and striking, but there were multitudes of delicate bluebells, and there were wild peony and "popcorn" and dainty snowdrops and "little Johnnies" and many more.

Raymond is a half wild little village with some fine rough hills and ravines about, but no sign of grand mountains or big trees or charming waterfalls. The Yosemite was still distant a two days' stage drive. It was the opening of the season and visitors were few. Only two others went on when I did. They were an elderly man and wife. But the stage also carried several men who were going to the Valley to work, one of them a Chinaman cook, another a blacksmith known as "Hank," and a third whom his comrades addressed as "Bud." The stage was a three-seated top wagon, and I sat on the front seat between the driver and the blacksmith.

Hour after hour we went on climbing among the rough, stony hills. They were not very interesting. Everywhere were granite boulders and scattered oaks garlanded with mistletoe, and now and then would occur a scrawny pine. In places there was much undergrowth such as sagebrush, chaparral, buckeye, and a bushy lupine that was loaded with purple blossoms. Then, too, there were great patches of poison oak, each shrub a reddish mass of new foliage. "You want to be careful how you walk through that," advised the driver; "though some people ain't affected by it at all. It don't trouble me none, and I've monkeyed with it for forty years—walked through it, handled it, and even had it in my mouth."

Grass was so plentiful that the driver remarked, "I would just like to be a cow for the next three months. I'd be sure to have all I wanted to eat, and I'd have nothing to do only to lie around. But by the end of June the grass will be dried brown, and the pasturing won't be so pleasant. Still, that brown grass ain't bad; for it's like hay and is all right till we have rains to wash the goodness out. We are likely to get wet weather in October, and then the cattle have a hard time. But if the rains come early in the fall the new grass soon starts. If the rains are late the dry feed is destroyed and the new doesn't get a chance to take its place. So the cattle half starve all winter."

In the valleys were occasional little farms or the homes of ranchmen, and presently the elderly man on the back seat pointed to one of these and said, "It seems to me that the people who live there must lead a lonely life."

"Oh, no," responded the driver, "they can drive to town in forty minutes; but then, they don't go there very often

because they're afraid of the cars."

We frequently saw birds. red-headed woodpeckers were working away on the dead trees and the telegraph poles, and blue jays and linnets were common. Once I got a glimpse of a robin, and there were a few hawks and soaring 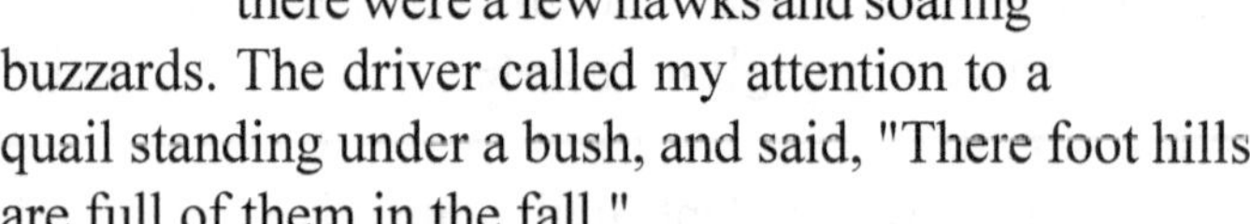 buzzards. The driver called my attention to a quail standing under a bush, and said, "There foot hills are full of them in the fall."

Several times we had a momentary glimpse of a ground squirrel scudding to shelter. The blacksmith claimed these squirrels were good to eat, but the driver declared they were no better than rats.

"Well," said the blacksmith, "cook 'em properly and they're good enough for anybody."

"Some people eat rattlesnakes," observed the driver.

"If I was going to eat one I'd want to kill it myself," the blacksmith said. "You know if you only just wound one it will bite itself where it was hurt and fill its flesh full of poison,"

In a number of spots along the way were rubbish dumps of dirt and broken stone where some old gold mine had been worked, and the lady passenger

wished she could get out and hunt for a "nudget." We passed through Grub Gulch which contains a mine still in operation, and in the rough mountain hollow was a rude little hamlet. The mine is not of much account, but in the booming days that followed its discovery, there was a wild and lawless community here. "They used to have a man for breakfast every little while," declared the driver.

Now and then we met a team, and among the rest were several wagons loaded with apples that

left a trail of delicious fragrance behind them. Later we saw the orchards in the secluded mountain glens, and I asked the driver if the fruit was profitable. He said, "That depends on the man who raises it and on circumstances. The fellow that handles this orchard we are passing has hard scratching to make ends meet, and he's close as a mosquito, too; but some do very well."

Much of the way the road clung to a steep hillside. It was narrow and crooked, and on the outer side looked dangerously precipitous. When teams approached each other, the drivers shouted a warning and were apt to stop to consider just how to pass. The broadest place possible was selected and one team crowded up to the bank while the other drove gingerly along on the verge. Our own experience was mild compared with what it would have been later in the

season when the five-span freighting wagons were running.

We were constantly encountering streams. They were seldom bridged and we splashed straight across. It was a pleasure to see them, for they were not

like the muddy streams of the lowlands, but were clear and sweet, with stone-strewn courses down which they leaped and foamed with unceasing melody. The road was more or less muddy, but the driver assured us that the first thirty miles of our journey were decidedly pleasanter than they would be in summer. Then there would be dust and torrid heat. "Why," said he, "it gets so hot that the wagon tongues hang out. I've seen the thermometer up to 118 in the shade."

One of the things that adds zest to the stage trip is the possibility of a hold-up. In the past, these hold-ups have occurred about once in four years. The previous season a highwayman had relieved a load of tourists of their purses, but did not take their jewelry or watches. He apologized for the annoyance he was causing and said he didn't like to have to resort to such a practice, but he needed the money.

When the collection had been finished, an English tourist got out his camera and said to the desperado, "I'd like to take your picture, you know."

"Certainly, go ahead," he replied, and then

submitted to the photographing very gracefully and departed.

The hold-up that preceded this one was an affair of more consequence. There were five stages going up the valley that day, one behind another, and a single man held them all up right in a bunch. He was a little particular, and when he thought a man had not turned over to him as much money as he carried, he ordered his victim to "dig up some more." But he was not without a touch of ceremonial politeness, for he presented each of his benefactors with his card on which was printed the words, "The Black Kid." At length, his work was completed and he took to the brush and was seen no more.

We stopped once in ten or twelve miles to change horses, but this made little delay as the horses were harnessed and waiting for us. The longest pause was twenty minutes at the station where we had our noon lunch. After this lunch, the blacksmith, as he settled himself in his place, smacked his lips and declared that the cream pie he had eaten for dessert was the finest pie of any sort he had ever tasted. "The only fault I have to find," said he in conclusion, "is that the cook is too good a mathematicianer and cuts his pies into too many pieces."

By mid-afternoon we had passed the foothills, and ahead of us lay a mountain. Bud informed the driver that he was going to get out and "hike" for a while, and when he alighted the blacksmith and I joined him. The trees had become more numerous and there were many tall, handsome yellow pines. Bushes were fewer, but in places the ground was hidden by a low evergreen growth of bear clover.

"The bears don't eat it," said the blacksmith, "but it smells like 'em."

"Seems to me," said Bud, "it smells just like a wet dog, and if you walk through it for an hour or two in summer you'll have that smell on your clothes for the rest of your life."

Just then the blacksmith found a horseshoe in the road and he hung it up on a bush. "That'll bring me good luck," he remarked.

"I don't know about that," was Bud's comment. "I've quit hangin' 'em up lately because I noticed I got drunk as a lord every time I did it."

As we climbed upward, the ground became increasingly muddy and slippery, and at length patches of snow were to be seen here and there in the woodland. These were larger and more frequent as we went higher until the mantle of white was everywhere. The sky had gloomed over and it began to storm, a moisture of rain and sleet. Now we arrived at a rough shanty and barn where the stage was to change horses. What a wintry wilderness it was!—white roofs and a giant evergreen forest roundabout, gloomy and mysterious with the cold storm.

When the stage came, we walkers got in and

tucked the blankets tightly about us and everyone prepared for a disagreeable journey; but shortly the mists drifted away and the sun shone into the shaggy, dripping woodland, and brightened the dark foliage and the brown, rough-barked tree trunks. The driver seemed anxious about his return trip on the morrow. "Gee! this snow'll be frozen then," he said, "and it'll be slick as glass. The brakes won't hold and I'll have a lot o' trouble to keep the wagon from runnin' onto the horses."

We presently passed over the top of the mountain ridge and were in really magnificent forest that man had never devastated. The trees grew to full maturity and died and fell to enrich the mountain mould for future generations just as their ancestors had before them from time immemorial. Many of the sugar and yellow pines and cedars were four to six feet in diameter, and they often towered up fully two hundred feet. It was a satisfaction just to look at their straight

and towering boles.

The noblest of the trees and those most prized by the lumbermen were the sugar pines. Specimens have been found that had attained a thickness of twelve feet and were still living, sound in every fiber. The cones are very large and handsome. They grow to be from a foot to eighteen inches long and beautify the tree and ground beneath for months after the seeds have taken wing. The tree's name comes from a sweet gum that exudes from the heart-wood where wounds have been made either by forest fires or the ax. The gum takes the shape of irregular, crisp clusters of kernels. When fresh it is perfectly white and delicious.

In descending the mountain, it was quite necessary to hole on. The wheels cut through the snow in a very uncertain way, and we thumped and jolted and shook about in a manner that was very disturbing. The lady on the seat behind was constantly cautioning her husband to hang on to her, even if her arm was getting blistered with his clutch. When her side of the vehicle tipped up, she begged him to hurry and shift as near her end of the seat as possible to keep the balance. When it went the other way, she had him slide back to his side. Yet in spite of all he could do to act as ballast, she was certain at times we were going over.

"Oh, oh!" she exclaimed as we passed safely through one crisis, "what foolishness to come all this way and over such poor and dangerous roads just to see a little scenery that we may not care for after all! I told you we would regret it, but you were bound to come."

Once when the driver let the horses break into a trot along the verge of a precipice, she ordered him to "Stop!" and added in an aside that she had never seen such reckless driving. Gradually we had left the snow behind and now we were much of the time dragging along in the mud. Darkness came, but at last we saw the lights of the tiny settlement of Wawona ahead and came out into a clearing in the valley basin, and there was our hotel with shelter and warmth and food.

The ground was stiff with frost the next morning, the air crisp and clear. We were on the road at seven and were soon climbing another mountain, snugging along the slope and creeping in and out of the ravines. Deer tracks were frequent in the highway mud, and these set the Yosemite workers who were on the stage to telling their experiences in hunting the animals, and they pointed out this place and that along the trail where they had shot one or more. We were on a government reservation where hunting was against the law, and from May to October a hundred of Uncle Sam's cavalry were stationed at Wawona to see that the law was enforced. But after the cavalry left, the huntsmen banged away very much as they pleased. While the soldier guardians were present they exercised some degree of restraint, yet the efficiency of the troops was generally rated pretty low.

According to a state official whose headquarters were in the Yosemite, the soldiers were worse than useless. "I'll give you an instance," he said. "Five soldiers caught one of the fellows that lives in these parts out hunting and they started for camp with him. But on the way, a deer crossed their trail and every one of the soldiers shot at it and missed.

" 'Give me my gun,' said the prisoner, 'and I'll kill the deer for you, if you want me to.'

"So they gave him his gun and he brought down

the deer," continued the official, "and then told him he could keep his gun and hike out.

"Yes, sir, these soldiers kill any quantity of game and they've fished out every stream and lake in this region. Before them Arabs got in here, we had some of the finest fishing in the Sierras

"Once the captain told me he was going to bring his cavalry up to camp in the Valley. Him and I locked horns right there and the soldiers didn't come. Thunder and lightning! I have no use for their sort, and there's too much red tape and pompousness about the whole management. The captain has got to come down off the roost if he wants to do business with me. Any bulldozing proposition won't go.

"We had a fire on the reservation last summer and it burned for six weeks and ran over a territory thirty-five square miles. For the whole six weeks, the Valley was full of smoke, and the tourists who came didn't get to see hardly anything at all. The fire very near burned up the soldiers' camp. They were supposed to be fighting the fire, but what class of persons are they? A fellow with any ginger in him wouldn't take a job at thirteen dollars a month. They aren't in the army to work. They know how to beat the game from A to Z, and for accomplishing anything really effective, they're no earthly use. Their police duty is a farce. Why, they're constantly getting drunk at Wawona and raising thunder. They make a regular scat-house of the place. This fire I was speaking of was altogether too much for them. They didn't know how to handle it, and they didn't care to exert themselves much anyhow. It's said that some of them would burn a space around themselves and then lie down and have a sleep. By and by the fire got up into my region and I took ten men and in three days put the whole thing out. With a dozen of these California foothill boys, I can do everything five hundred of the soldiers and a brigadier-general in command of 'em could do, and a blamed sight better. They are supposed to keep  cattle and sheep off the reservation, but there's men who will feed a flock of sheep all around those soldiers. Give me a few local rangers and I'd nab every herder that sticks his nose across the line. Geewhizacar! I'd catch more trespassers in six months than they would in a hundred years."

The stage toiled on till we were again in the white winter woods. As we climbed higher, the snow grew deeper and in some places a passage had been shoveled through, leaving walls on either side half-way to the top of the stage. Finally, we reached a little station over six thousand feet above the sea level. It was in a small clearing, with the dark, serrated woods all

about, and it was fairly buried in drifts eight or ten feet deep. A narrow channel had been dug, and a little space cleared before the barn. We ate a hasty lunch and were soon on the road again, wallowing through the snow and pitching about in the most exciting manner, always with a vague fear that the vehicle might chance to turn over and send us to destruction down the mountain side.

In time, we came to where we could look down on the famous Valley—a long winding crevice bounded by mighty cliffs and peaks of many varying forms. How quiet and protected it did look after all those savage, inhospitable heights and hollows we had traversed! But the thing that made it most attractive was a slender waterfall dropping over the face of one of the giant bluffs—dainty, fairy-like and giving the otherwise sober landscape a touch of lightness that was very fascinating. This fall was the keynote of the scene through all the long descent to the valley bottom. It was the Bridalveil, dashing down for nine hundred feet, a mass of foam and spray, and as we drew near we saw shreds of rainbow painting the mists. The driver pointed out another waterfall across the valley, but a

very tiny one, which he said was called "The Maiden's Tear."

"That's a very curious name," said the lady passenger. "Why do they call it that?"

"Because it is so far from the Bridalveil," replied the driver.

The Valley is about seven miles long and nowhere much exceeds a mile in width. Nearly all of it is perfectly level, some of it open meadows and

pastures, but mostly thinly wooded with tall pines and cedars and firs intermingled with occasional deciduous trees or groves. A small river, rapid and rocky and crystal clear, wended its way through the vale, and, all along, the great cliffs soared skyward in many a vast buttress and pinnacle. It was a wilderness valley, and

yet it was so level and secluded and so hedged about by protecting mountains that it seemed a spot of eternal calm and serenity.

The Yosemite was first seen by white men in

January, 1851. For some time previous, there had been friction with the Indians on the mountain borders, but the first serious quarrel occurred when six Indians visited a trading post thirty miles west of the Valley, and a drunken ruffian from Texas, without any reasonable cause, stabbed to the heart the chief of the party. The other five Indians at once shot the Texan to death with their bows and arrows, and retreated to the forest. Two nights later a pack of sixteen mules was stolen from the trading post corral by the Indians and driven off to the mountains.

These happenings occasioned great excitement among the whites. It was midwinter, yet a company of about one hundred men from the vicinity armed

themselves and started on the trail. The Indians had gone to the Yosemite canyon where they converted the mules into jerked meat, and there the frontiersmen surprised them and slaughtered a large number. It was a massacre that included men, women and children. The whites were revenged and they left the Valley.

Although this group that pursued the Indians

were the first to see the famous spot, it was only made known to the outside world by an expedition that went on a similar raid two months later. Those who took part in the second foray had a rough time in the snowstorms and deep drifts of the mountains, and when they reached the Valley they found no Indians except one old woman. However, the scenery so impressed certain member of the party that their descriptions of it aroused very wide interest in its marvels.

The Valley is supposed to have been given its peculiar character by a convulsion that caused the rock mass filling the space to sink to some unknown depth. For a vast period of time, the waste from the side of the cliffs dropped into this abyss, which was doubtless occupied by a lake of surpassing beauty. But at length the hollow was filled sufficiently by the falling rocks and by the soil the streams brought from the regions surrounding so that the lake became the present alluvial valley.

Half way up the glen is a village consisting of a two-story wooden hotel and its annexes and several photograph studios, a store, a tiny church and a few dwellings. The hamlet looked strangely lost with the tremendous heights towering

around. Just beyond a meadow the Yosemite fall drops over from the crest of a rock wall twenty-six hundred feet high. How slender and beautiful it is, and how amazing its long leap! It brightens the whole vicinity and relieves the somberness of the ragged mountainous cliffs, and the air resounds with its mellow roar. It is characteristic of the canyon that you have the music of the waterfalls in your ears wherever you go, while the great rock walls loom about with a constantly changing sky-line. Of course, not all visitors are satisfied, and one man said to me, "These mountains around the Valley are all right, but I don't think much of the waterfalls, after seeing Niagara."

As well say a hummingbird is not beautiful because you have seen an eagle.

Up at the far end of the Valley where it narrows

and you look ahead into a wild wooded defile, is Mirror Lake. This, however, scarcely deserves its name for the only time it is apt to be quiet is before sunrise. Soon afterward the wind sucks down the Valley and the surface is broken with waves for the rest of the day.

Trails lead to the top of all the important bluffs and peaks, and it would seem as if a person could climb to his heart's content. But to some people a trail is too prosaic and they like the glory of going up where there are difficulties and danger. In a recent summer, an old alpine climber named Bailey and a young companion decided to follow up a steep crevice along the wall of El

Capitan to the summit of that king of cliffs. It proved a very arduous task, and the younger man several times urged the elder to return, but the latter was determined to go on. They were nearly to the top, and Bailey, who was ahead, sat down on a ledge and reached his staff to assist his comrade. Suddenly he toppled over and bounded along down the rocky slope. The young man saw him disappear, and to calm his nerves he seated himself and smoked a cigarette. He did not dare to descend, and when he rose he struggled up to the summit and followed the trail down to the hotel. Helpers promptly returned with him carrying a number of long ropes, and after a good deal of difficulty, they recovered the body of Bailey about seven hundred feet below where he fell.

The winter residents of the Valley number only about thirty, but in summer the village expands wonderfully. Hundreds of tents are put up to serve as

homes for campers and the place is very populous. Formerly this was a "tin can town" just as are most California hamlets—that is, the street and neighborhood were strewn with the rusty receptacles of canned goods which enter largely into the Western bill of fare. But now every dweller, temporary or permanent, is compelled to bury his old tins. It seems a pity that the buildings should be so uncomely and cheap, and one regrets the ugly wooden or iron bridges, so artificial and out of keeping with the landscape. The bridges might well be arches of the native stone, simple and permanent, that would make the scenes of which they are a part more beautiful instead of less so.

When my visit came to an end and I rode out of the Yosemite, it was with many a lingering and half-regretful backlook as we climbed the mountain and left behind that vale of enchantment with its mighty environing heights and delectable waterfalls. Two ladies sat on the box seat with the driver, who was unusually youthful, intelligent and entertaining. They were discussing the timidity of travelers, and the driver said, "I have had ladies riding on this seat, who, when the wagon gave a bad jolt, would holler and grab hold of me."

"You liked that, didn't you?" said the lady next to him.

"Well, not while I was drivin'," he responded. "I wouldn't object some other times, perhaps."

"I suppose you do have some funny people on the stage, the lady remarked."

"Yes," he said, "there was a trip last summer I carried a load that was all women, and every one of 'em

was an old maid, and always would be. The youngest of the lot must have been thirty-five or forty."

"That's not so very old," the lady interrupted. "There's plenty of chances for her yet."

"Well," was the driver's response, "all I can say is, if she's goin' to marry she'd better get a move on her.

"Those old maids was at me to tell 'em a story, or give 'em a conundrum, and finally I says, 'Why is it that an old maid likes to go to church early?' They couldn't tell, and I said, 'Because she wants to be sure to be there when the hymns are given out.' They said I was awful to give such a conundrum as that, but it pleased 'em all the same."

"Were those old maids from the East?" inquired the lady.

"Yes, there ain't none out here," replied the driver. "Our girls all marry, and there's not enough to go around."

"You are not married, are you?" queried the lady.

"Oh, I was taken long ago," he responded. "Get

up, Humpy, go on Smoke!" he said, cracking his whip over the backs of the front horses.

"What are the names of the other two?" the lady questioned.

"Coon and Toothpick," he replied.

Each of the three hundred and fifty horses on the route has its name and its individuality, but I think the names of our four had more than the average of picturesqueness.

From Wawona, where we arrived in the afternoon, I made a side trip to see the big trees. This necessitated an eight-mile climb up a mountain side for the trees love a high altitude. The road had only just been opened through the snows, and once our stage got stuck in a drift. Considerable digging had to be done before the struggling horses could drag us free. As we were toiling slowly along, the driver asked us if we had ever seen one of their black California rabbits. We never had.

"Why, there's one now," he said, pointing on ahead.

Sure enough, there was the rabbit sitting on its haunches alert and watchful close by the road, and it was nearly three feet tall. I expected every moment it would leap away, but we continued to approach and it did not move except that I saw an eye blink and its ears waggle a trifle. We were all very much excited over the sight and were exclaiming softly to one another when lo! we suddenly realized that the rabbit was nothing but a remnant of a burned-out stump that chanced from a certain viewpoint to have the outline of a rabbit.

When we were well up on the height, we changed to a sleigh and at last we came to the forest giants. They are in the midst of heavy woodland and are scattered among trees of various other species, any of which are themselves of magnificent girth and height, but the sequoias stand out distinctly. Their reddish brown bark is unlike the bark of the rest of the trees in texture as well as color, and the larger trees far exceed in size any of the comrades not of the same family. They differ also from the balance of the forest in having dome-like tops instead of pointed ones. Most of them are sadly scarred about the base by fire, but the

charred crevices and hollows date far back and are said to be due to the habit the Indians had of letting fires run through the woodland to clear it of undergrowth and make easier travelling and hunting.

The most venerable and the largest member of the clan is the "Grizzly Giant." It is supposed to be over five thousand years old, and its immense size, its shattered and dead top and gnarled limbs make it look like the ancestor of its race. The tree is ninety-three feet in circumference, and its first limb, a hundred feet from the ground, has a diameter of six feet. Many of the sequoias have broken and bare tops, but this is the work of storms rather than age. Even when a big tree falls, the end is still far off for the wood does not decay readily at heart, and the wasting away from the outside is very slow. Trees that were thrown down before the Pilgrims landed at Plymouth Rock are in the Sierra forests today with wood in them as sound and bright in color as it was in their prime. Most full-grown trees are not much over twenty feet in diameter and about two hundred and seventy-five feet in height. But the giants of the race go up fifty feet more. The trees, except for accidents, seem to lack little of being immortal. They live on indefinitely until cast down by storms, burned, killed by lightning or destroyed by man.

The fruitfulness of the sequoias is marvelous. The cones are only about two inches in length but the branches hang full of them and each is packed with two or three hundred seeds. Millions of seeds are ripened annually by a single tree—no doubt, enough in some cases to plant all the mountain ranges in the world. However, very few seeds ever get the chance to germinate, and of those that do, not one tree in ten thousand lives through the vicissitudes that beset its youth. Yet trees abound of all ages, from fresh-starting saplings to those in the glory of their prime, and the giant trees seem abundantly able to maintain their race in eternal vigor.

The day following this visit to the big trees, I returned to Raymond, and it was not so prosaic a change from the wonderland where I had been as might have been expected. Indeed, it was a real delight to descend from the wintry mountains and to gradually find the spring about us—at first only faint hints, but finally a green earth, and new leafage on the trees and abounding blossoms, and the birds flitting and singing.

Notes:

The word Yosemite means "full grown grizzly bear." Since 1905, the park has been in the charge of the federal government and is policed by two troops of cavalry who camp near the Yosemite Fall. This waterfall is the highest in the world with anything like the same amount of water. When it comes over the top of the cliffs, it is about thirty-five feet wide. A splendid ice-cone, five hundred feet high, forms at the foot of the upper fall in winter. [Editor's annotation: It is now more generally accepted that the word Yosemite comes from Miwok terms referring to a fierce tribe that lived in the Valley. Yohhe'meti (Southern Miwok) or Yos s e'meti (central Miwok) means "those who kill." The two terms are somewhat similar to those for grizzly bear and were confused by early interpreters.

Reference: Dr. Madison Scott Beeler. "Yosemite and Tamalpais." *Names: A Journal of Onomastics*. 3, no. 3 (1955): 185-186, as cited and noted by Daniel E. Anderson in "Origin of the Word Yosemite," *Yosemite Online* (2004).]

Bridalveil Fall derives its name from the effect on it of the wind, which often makes it flutter like a filmy veil.

Travelers now usually go to the Valley by way of Merced and El Portal. From the latter place, where the railroad ends, a twelve-mile stage road takes one into the heart of the Valley.

The Yosemite season lasts from early April until October, though it is now possible to go at any time without serious discomfort. The cold, and the heavy snowfall on the mountains are the chief deterrents to winter visits. The best months are May and June when the falls are full of water and there is no dust.

The customary way to see the famous Mariposa grove of Big Trees now is to make an excursion from the Yosemite Valley. It is twenty-six miles to the hotel at Wawona, and eight miles more to the grove. Here are about six hundred fine specimens of the sequoia.

The situation of San Francisco makes it a logical metropolis. It has one of the largest harbors in the world, and there is no other that can in the least rival this between San Diego and Puget Sound. Besides, the bay and its rivers give an admirable opportunity for extensive and cheap water commerce inland, and the great fertile valleys which open away toward the interior are naturally tributary to the city that guards the Golden Gate. The city is built on about a dozen hills which add greatly to its picturesqueness. It turns its back on the sea, and its wharves front the bay easterly. The name which designates the passage from the Pacific into the harbor was applied by Fremont in 1848, and has nothing to do with the gold-bearing districts. "Golden" referred to the fertility of the country on the shores of the bay.

The settlement of the place dates back to 1776 when the Franciscan Friars established a Mission here. The Mission was in the center

of the peninsula, halfway between the sea and the harbor. For over fifty years it was the nucleus of quite a village, and the community in its prime had a population of five hundred Indians and Mexicans. Another settlement was presently established on the shore of the bay for commercial purposes and came to have a considerable trade in hides and tallow.

In January 1848, James W. Marshall discovered gold while digging a ditch for a sawmill about forty-five miles northeast of Sacramento. This caused tremendous excitement in San Francisco and two thirds of the population left for the new region of promise. Lots in the city sold for one half what they

were worth a month before, but the necessities of life began to get scarce in the gold camps, and some of the miners returned to San Francisco and prepared to profit through the rapid increase of business that was sure to come. The large finds of gold in the interior brought an inrush of newcomers and the population early in 1849 was two thousand. By July it was five thousand, and this number doubled the following year. Between April and December 1849 over five hundred vessels arrived bringing thirty-five thousand passengers. As many more immigrants came overland, but the great majority found their way with little delay to the mines. Such was the eagerness to share in the golden fortune that scores of vessels lay in the harbor unable to proceed farther for want of sailors because the crews had deserted in a body almost as soon as the anchors were dropped. Some of these vessels eventually rotted where they were moored. Others were hauled up on the beach to serve as storehouses, lodging-houses and saloons. For a long time, several of them, flanked by buildings and wharves and forming part of a street, were original features of the town.

Money in the period of sudden growth was scarce, and gold dust was the principal medium of exchange. During 1848 the monthly yield of gold in California averaged three hundred thousand dollars, in 1849 a million and a half, in 1850 three million. Prices of labor and all supplies were very high. Flour was forty dollars a barrel, butter ninety cents a pound, a loaf of bread fifty cents, a hard-boiled egg one dollar. A tin pan or a wooden bowl cost five dollars, and a pick or a shovel ten dollars. But laborers received a dollar an hour, and in spite of the cost of living, everybody made money.

Bayard Taylor who visited San Francisco at this time says that, "Around the curve of the bay hundreds of tents and houses appeared, scattered all over the heights and along the shore for more than a mile. On every side stood buildings begun or half finished, and the greater part of them were canvas sheds open in front and with signs in all languages. Great quantities of goods were piled in the open air for want of a place to store them. The streets were full of people hurrying to and fro and of as diverse and bizarre a character as the houses."

The winter season of 1849 and 1850 was very rainy, and the streets, which had not as yet been either graded or paved, became simply impassable. In many places, wagons would sink to the wheel-hubs, and the animals were sometimes so deeply mired they could not be extricated and were left to die where they were. Trees and shrubbery and boxes and barrels of goods were thrown into the streets to afford a passage-way.

The city continued its rapid growth, and by 1853 the population had increased to forty-two thousand. With the influx of treasure-seekers came a motley crowd of adventurers from all points on the Pacific Coast, Australia and the East, and many of them made a living by preying on their fellows. Gambling jumped into popular favor, and though stringent measures were adopted for its abatement they did not avail. Fortunes were made and lost in a single day, and many a miner who came from the interior to embark for his home, by trying to increase his fortune at the gaming table found himself penniless and obliged to return to the mines and begin all over.

There were parts of the city where even a policeman hardly dared to go, and night was made hideous with debauchery and assaults. During the early years of the city's awakening many murders were committed by the desperadoes, yet no one was hanged for the crimes, and the courts became a byword. The situation was intolerable and in 1851 the famous Vigilance Committee was organized in the interests of law and order. This committee within a month tried and hanged four men and banished thirty others, and the course pursued was universally upheld by public opinion. Conditions became normal and the committee ceased its labors. But in 1856 crime had once more become rampant and the law impotent. The vigilantes reorganized and acted with the same vigor and with the same results as before, and there was again individual security and public order.

The history of San Francisco's beginnings is extremely interesting to anyone who visits the city and these strange happenings and conditions form a fascinating background. They were constantly in my mind when I was there early in 1906 and added much to the significance of what I saw. For a place of its size I was surprised to find so much of it built of wood. Of course certain fine residences and many of the big business blocks were of material more permanent and substantial, but even in the commercial heart of the town wooden structures were plentiful, while in the residence sections redwood dwellings were almost universal. I wondered what would happen if a big fire got started and mentioned this thought to a native. He, however, assured me that I need have no apprehension on that score for they had the finest fire department in the world, and no fire could get beyond control.

Another feature of the city that engaged my attention was its weather. Someone had told me that, "with its rains and fogs and rough winds San Francisco has about the meanest climate that ever a man set foot in." I suppose there is a modicum of truth in the statement, but during my stay the weather was rather fine. If we had rain it came at night, and though there was often fog and gloom in the early morning the sun presently broke through. Then followed a period of dreamy calm, but later the wind came blustering in from the sea and for much of the afternoon blew with uncomfortable violence. This seemed to be the daily program.

The city's fame as a seaport drew me early to the wharves. Everywhere here for miles were ships loading and unloading, and I found toil and din and smoke and dubious smells no matter whither I wandered. Against the sky was a dense forest of tapering masts with their network of rigging, and here and there were stout steamer funnels belching soot and fumes. The great drays banged and rattled along over the rough pavements, there was clanking of chains, the panting of engines, the shouts of men. Loafers strolled about or roosted on piles of boards and other chance seats, and children and sightseers mingled with the rest of the crowds, all drawn by the allurement of the sea-going ships and the varied activity. It was a rude region, and the business buildings which fronted toward the wharves were dingy and forbidding. Saloons were predominant, and these endeavored to interest the public by the individuality of their names, as for instance, the North Pole, the Castle, the Tea Cup, Life Saving Station and Thirst Parlor, The Fair Wind, and Jim's Place.

Whatever else the stranger in San Francisco missed seeing he was sure to visit the Chinese quarter. Here was an oriental community of fifteen thousand in the heart of the city. It occupied an area of about ten square blocks. No space was wasted, and besides the main thoroughfares, there were many narrow byways running in all directions and lined with little places of business. Often the buildings were curiously ornamented and made resplendent with many colored paints and big paper lanterns, but the majority were battered and aged and grimy.

The first Chinese to arrive in California came on the brig Eagle in February 1848. They were two men and one woman. Within the next two years about five hundred came, and by 1852 there were eighteen thousand. Large numbers went direct to the mines where they worked for a few cents a day. The enmity aroused by their competition in the labor market resulted in exclusion laws, and latterly their numbers have been decreasing. Naturally, therefore, the racial bitterness which the Americans have felt toward the Mongolians is somewhat allayed. Yet harsh feeling is still to be encountered, and one man enlightened me thus:

"They ought to be kept out—every one of 'em. Go to the farming country and watch how they manage on their ranches workin' all the time, night and day, and Sundays, rain or shine. A white man has no show against them—not a particle. When it comes to disposing of what he raises, the Chinaman sells every time he starts out to make a trade. Ask him the price of a bunch of beets.

" 'Five cents,' he says.

" 'Too much,' you say.

"He picks up another bunch and says, 'Here, two bunches for five cents today,' and you take them.

"A Chinaman knows how to accumulate the cash. He will come into this country with nothing and go away with a bag of money as long as your arm.

"In the city they crowd into the smallest quarters and eat the cheapest food. They are a thrifty people and an honest people, I'll say that for them. They stand by their bargains and always pay when they say they'll pay. I'd rather sell goods to a Chinese merchant than an American so far as finance goes. Some are millionaires. But they don't help develop the country. They don't invest here. All their money, sooner or later, goes back to China, and it's a big drain.

"That ain't where we're goin' to get hit the worst, though. The Chinese who do us the most harm are those that come to look around or to study. You see the Chinese are cracker-jacks to imitate. Give 'em the chance and they'd take all our ideas about machinery and how to do things in a modern way. Then they'd go back to China and start their manufactories, and we wouldn't be in it at all."

I found a few of the Chinatown shops large and fine, and the goods in them were often expensive, rare, and delightfully original and charming in design. But for the most part the shops were small and not by any means prepossessing. Usually they had open fronts, and much of the stock was displayed on the sidewalk, and the walks were also made use of for the conducting of many minor industries such as cobbling and tinkering. I loitered about for hours watching the strange scenes. The people with their yellow visages and unfamiliar garments looked as if they had been exhumed from some prehistoric past. The men mostly wore black or dark blue. Often the women wore these colors likewise, but a good many had clothing as

gay as a rainbow, and so did the children. The women went about bareheaded and their garments consisted of large loose-fitting blouses with huge sleeves and a pair of trousers of equally generous proportions.

The inhabitants included some persons of refinement and learning, and a considerable number of keen and successful businessmen, but the larger part were of the lower class. This, I suppose, is the reason why the women usually had normal feet, yet once in a while I saw one stump along with feet that seemed to be non-existent.

In various places were walls pasted over with hieroglyphic notices and bulletins, nearly all printed on red or yellow paper, and the passers often paused to read. There was always an absorbed group in front of a trinket stand where some colored Japanese battle pictures were displayed. No space in the buildings was wasted, and the occupants were much given to burrowing about underground. The filth of the basements had formerly been superlative, but of late, by order of the city, every cellar had been supplied with a cement floor. The shopkeepers seemed very busy, yet sometimes I would see one taking his ease and smoking his long pipe in contemplative peace and satisfaction, or I would see a group standing about a table at the back of their cavernous little place of business eating with their chopsticks and drinking tea. Every butcher had an entire roasted hog hung up from which he cut portions as they were wanted. Some of the meat and dried fish and vegetables looked very uncanny. I often could not tell what the things were, but I did recognize on sale in one shop a chicken's feet minus the skin.

Almost every kind of business was represented in Chinatown. They even had a bookstore, and they published a daily newspaper. Barbers' shops were numerous, for every man had his head shaved about once a week, and when you looked into the tonsorial establishment you perhaps saw the barber making the job thorough by shaving the inside of the subject's ears. One very busy alley was largely given up to the sale of fish. The stores were full of the finny merchandise, the narrow walks were almost covered, and numerous great shallow baskets spread with fish, and crabs and clams were put on boxes along the curb at either side of the street.

I went into a joss-house. In the lower room was a group of men smoking (and gambling, so I was told). Up above was the room of worship, gorgeous but tawdry. It was crowded with paraphernalia and well supplied with wooden images. Nearby was a fine restaurant occupying an entire building. The furnishings were very aristocratic, and there was much carving and heavy oriental chairs and tables. It was run by a company of eight men, and their safe in one corner of an eating apartment had eight padlocks on it. Each partner carried the key to his individual padlock, and the safe could only be opened when all were present.

Another place I visited was the underground shop of an "inventor," as he called himself. But his inventions were more curious than original. They were all rather rude mechanisms that did things of no particular use. One of the oddest was an arrangement for reading by candlelight. When you were through you let go of your book which was hitched to a string from above, and it was drawn up out of the way. At the same time the candle swung back and an extinguisher dropped over it.

A somewhat similar subterranean shop was occupied by a very old man who had two mimic theatres fastened to his wall crowded with actors, one-half life size. He would set the mechanism going and the figures would bob their heads and move their hands in a most unearthly manner. He also had a wonder-stone, a polished disc about eighteen inches across and with many smoky stains in the rock. The old man pointed out in the stains a great number of figures—men, women and animals—but it was seldom I would make out the things he said he saw.

There were pawn-shops in Chinatown, and in the windows you were sure to see, among other articles, several opium pipes. Opium is less used than formerly, but opium dens still existed, and I wandered into one of them. Its entrance was at the back of a gloomy hallway. Within was a large apartment having a double tier of platforms at the sides on which were heaps of blankets and a few Chinamen sleeping or smoking. One ancient was lying on his side and toasting a bit of opium on the end of a slender stick over a little lamp. Then he crowded it into the orifice of his pipe and puffed away. Another fellow was smoking a water-pipe—that is, drawing tobacco fumes through a one-inch tube, two feet long, filled with water. This individual showed me various small trinkets which he said were very cheap because they had been smuggled in from abroad by friends. The Chinaman is not very particular about obeying laws that he can evade. He even holds slaves—for one alley was pointed out where, behind barred windows, the women slaves of this strange community were kept.

My sojourn in San Francisco came to an end at length, and one evening in the early dusk I crossed the bay to go on by train to other regions. From the ferry-boat I looked back and saw the great city with its masts and towers and heights, gray and beautiful against the glow of the sunset sky. Lights were everywhere a-twinkle, and the beholder could not but be impressed with the greatness of the city—populous, rich, serene and powerful, and yet one week later came the great earthquake and the fire that reduced this metropolis of the west coast to a blackened ruin.

Notes:

The old San Francisco is no more, but the attraction of its situation will always remain, and the new tragedy in its stirring history adds greatly to the interest of the visitor. At about five o'clock of Wednesday morning, April 18, 1906, occurred the first great shock of that elemental calamity. It had been a beautiful night, and the Post-Lenten fever of society's revels was at its height. That night the climax of the Grand Opera season had been reached in a magnificent performance, and never before had there been such enthusiasm in San Francisco's musical world. The performance was only concluded at midnight, and then for hours the cafés had been gay with the laughter and discussions of the opera-goers. Even at the time of the great shock some of the revelers were still in the streets. There was a series of shuddering jerks and writhings of the earth, here and there a crash of falling walls, then a profound silence for several minutes. After that was heard the clangor of the gong on the cart of the fire chief as he dashed through the heart of the city. Broken gas-pipes had started fires, but worst of all, beneath the surface of the streets, the water mains had been severed, and the city was doomed. Not until three days later did the conflagration burn itself out. Over four square miles of the city were gone utterly, property to the value of more than a third of a billion dollars had been destroyed, and the larger portion of the inhabitants were homeless refugees in the public parks.

A new and more substantial city has risen from the ashes, and it continues, as before, to be the largest city on the Pacific Coast. It is at the north end of a long peninsula. On the west is the ocean and on the east is San Francisco Bay, fifty miles long and ten miles wide. The city lies mainly on the shore of the Bay and on the steep hills that rise a little back from the water's edge.

The Golden Gate which gives entrance from the sea to the Bay is one mile across. The Presidio, or Government Military Reservation, stretches along the Golden Gate for four miles. Daily drills of the troops stationed there are held from 9 to 11 a.m.

Beyond the Presidio, on the outermost portion of the peninsula that borders the Golden Gate, is the popular resort, Sutro Heights Park. A great attraction here is the view of the Seal Rocks. These rocks are three in number, conical in shape, and from twenty to fifty feet high, and only a stone's throw from the land.

On them huge sea lions bask in the sun. Some of the creatures weigh over half a ton and are from twelve to fifteen feet long. They are protected by law, and scores of them are always hovering about the rocks. Their evolutions in the water are very interesting, and their singular barking can be heard above the roar of the breakers. Nearby are swimming pools and an aquarium.

A little to the south is Golden Gate Park with its fine lawns, serpentine drives, shady walks, gorgeous flowers, and groves of tropical or semi-tropical trees, and its wonderful collection of animals and birds.

One of the most interesting historical relics of the city is the old Mission Dolores at the corner of Dolores and 16th streets. The superstitious believe that it escaped by divine intervention the great fire which destroyed so much of the city. It dates from about 1778. The adobe walls are three feet thick, it has a tile roof, and the floor is of earth except near the altar. Adjoining it is a neglected little churchyard.

The Chinese Quarter has been rebuilt since the fire, and is still one of the most fascinating features of the city. It contains about 10,000 inhabitants, mostly men.

The San Francisco climate is notably equable, without extremes of either cold or heat. Nevertheless, visitors should always have warm wraps available, for strong chilling winds from the sea are frequent even in summer.

Beyond the Golden Gate, northward, rises Mt. Tamalpais, 2600 feet high. A scenic railroad climbs to its summit, whence can be had an excellent view of the entire bay region.

At Berkeley, just across the bay from San Francisco, is the University of California, with its extensive and picturesque grounds. It has over 3,000 students, one-third of whom are women. An unusual feature of its equipment is an open-air Greek theater, which accommodates 12,000 spectators and is used for university meetings, commencement exercises and concerts.

Automobile trips can be made from San Francisco in every direction. One of the best roads is that to Sacramento, the capital of the state, 136 miles distant. Perhaps an even pleasanter way to make this trip is to go by steamer up the Sacramento River. Orchards and gardens are almost continuous along the banks of the stream.

The motorist going south from San Francisco will find good dirt roads in the main, but in places they are very narrow, and have some sharp turns and steep grades. Thirty-four miles takes one to Palo Alto. The name means tall tree, and the great redwood which suggested the name still stands. Stanford University is the great attraction at Palo Alto. It has an endowment of $30,000,000, and its buildings in the Mission style of architecture, with long corridors and inner courts, are the finest possessed by any university in the world.

Twenty miles farther south, is San José in the center of the largest compact orchard on the globe, sheltered by the mountains round about from every asperity of land or sea. This is the starting-point for Lick Observatory, twenty-six miles away on Mt. Hamilton. Stages make the round trip in a day, allowing an hour's stay on the mountain. The road is excellent, and the views are beautiful and ever-changing. The distance to the summit from the base of the mountain is only two miles in a direct line, but by the road it is seven miles. The road is said to make three hundred and sixty-five bends in this upward climb. The observatory is one of the most notable in the world in point of situation, equipment, and achievement. Its great telescope has a 36-inch object glass. James Lick, whose gift of $700,000 built the observatory, is buried in the foundation pier of the telescope.

Continuing the journey southward from Palo Alto, we reach Santa Cruz, ninety-one miles from San Francisco. This is a favorite summer and winter resort, with an excellent bathing beach, fine cliffs and good fishing. Six miles distant is a grove of big trees, about twenty of which have a diameter of over ten feet. One of them attains a diameter of twenty-three feet. A large hollow tree is shown in which General Fremont camped for several days in 1847.

Somewhat farther down the coast is charming Monterey, the old capital of California in the days of Spanish rule. Richard Henry Dana Jr., in his *Two Years Before the Mast*, describing Monterey as it was in 1835, before California had become a part of the United

States, says: "It makes a very pretty appearance; its houses being of whitewashed adobe. The red tiles, too, on the roofs contrast well with the white sides. There are no streets nor fences (except that here and there a small patch might be fenced in for a garden) so that the houses are placed at random. In the center of the place is an open square, surrounded by four lines of one-story buildings, with half a dozen cannon in the center, some mounted and others not. This is the presidio, or fort. Every California town has a presidio in its center, or rather every presidio has a town built around it, for the forts were first built by the Mexican government, and then the people built near them for protection.

AMONG THE SHASTA FOOTHILLS

It was eleven o'clock at night, and I had just stopped off at a little railway station in Northern California. The station was not lighted, and when the train rumbled away, I was left blinking in the uncertain darkness. I looked this way and that for some sign of habitation and saw none. Looming against the northern sky rose a grim black peak, an almost perfect pyramid, strangely regular and vast and near. In the east rose another pyramid mountain mass, ghostly white with eternal snows. That I knew was Shasta. I began exploring the lonely void around and presently discovered a man with a lantern on the other side of the station. This man was good enough to act as my guide, and he piloted me across the road to a story-and-a-half hotel hidden among some trees. Then he went his way. The building was dark and silent. I stepped up on the piazza and after rapping again and again without avail reinforced my blows with shouts of "Hello!"

At length, a woman's voice responded, and presently the lady of the house appeared with a candle. She said she had no accommodations left except a cot bed but, as her hotel was the only one in the hamlet, a cot bed seemed to me a very satisfactory solution of my difficulties. She gave me the candle, and I climbed a narrow stairway into a garret—a little, rough-boarded apartment with a closed deal door at either end and a rude railing around the stairway-opening in the middle. A stand and a chair were in one corner, and in each of the other corners was a cot bed. Two of the beds were already occupied. The other was mine. There were no windows and no provision for ventilation, and after I blew out the candle, the room was as dark as a pocket. Downstairs I could hear a clock solemnly ticking. One of my fellow-roomers was snoring uneasily, and the other would now and then talk in his sleep. But at last all this faded out of my consciousness, and when I awoke there were glints of light coming in at sundry cracks and knot holes in the partitions that separated the garret I was in from the apartments adjoining at either end. The occupants of these rooms were astir, and one at a time, two from each chamber, they entered my room and passed down the stairway.

My fellow-roomers now rose, and one of them, as he dressed, lit and smoked a cigarette. To wash we were obliged to go down to the back porch, where on a bench was a basin with a pail beside it from which to dip the necessary water. From this little porch, we had the mighty form of Shasta in full view, marvelous in the height of its aspiring pinnacles and in the unsullied whiteness with

which the snows clothed its wild crags. The woodland darkened its base, but the trees gradually frayed out and ceased long before they reached the summit.

We could also look forth from the porch on that near and frowning peak of gloom I had seen the night before. From bottom to top it was little else than barren rock and loose slides of stone. "It's called Black Butte," said the hired girl, "and I've been told it's infested with rattlesnakes, and that the rocks are all wore slick with the snakes comin' and goin'. It's a fine place for 'em all right, and people say if you go to the mountain just about sun-up you can see the rattlesnakes pokin' up their heads all around."

"Well," said the landlady, "I know that knoll on the east side of Black Butte is a regular rattlesnake den. I had a boarder once named Chapman, and he had a perfect mania for catchin' rattlesnakes. He was really luny about it, and he went after 'em every Sunday. I've never clumb up there, but I've seen the snakes' tracks crossin' the road down below. He'd catch 'em alive and ship 'em off and sell 'em."

"It's said that if you get a good fat rattlesnake

and try out the oil that oil is a wonderful cure for rheumatism," remarked one of the lodgers. "You rub it on and take it internally, both."

"I'm not scared of snakes," declared the hired girl, gazing meditatively at the dark stony height. "I'd just as soon tackle 'em as not, but I don't want anything to do with a mouse. Mice are creatures I can't stand. I can dance for a week if I see a mouse runnin' around the room. Yes, you bet I can!"

"I ain't stuck on seein' mice or snakes either," said the landlady, "but I think the varmints back on Shasta are worse than the snakes."

Then she told how, occasionally, a brown bear was captured and wildcats shot, and how right there at the hotel they sometimes would hear a California lion roar, or the coyotes yelping. In the midst of her observations she came to a sudden stop and chased out an old hen that had walked into the house and was looking around. "That there hen has got to change its habits!" she announced. "For two days it has laid an egg on my bed, and I won't have such doin's."

The hens were laying very well at present, she said, only they often stole nests off in the manzanita shrubs and thorny "sticker-bushes" where she could not find the eggs.

The place where I was stopping was a woodland mill village clustering about some big red box-factory buildings with their piles of boards. Some of the houses were substantial cottages, but most were little shacks of unplaned boards that in themselves and in their surroundings were extremely unprepossessing. Their occupants were mostly "Eye-talians." There were no gardens, no green grass-only ragged forest of brush and stumps and brown gritty earth. All the vicinity had been cleared of its good timber.

One odd feature of the village was its ovens. Under a shed adjoining nearly every house was a plank platform on which was built a dome-like cavern of stones and cement. In this a fire is made, and when it has burned down to embers it is raked out, and the loaves of bread are put in and the opening closed. The heat the oven has absorbed from the fire does the baking.

In my walks, I often heard the weird honking of wild geese, and when I turned my eyes upward I would see a flock of the great birds with outstretched necks winging their swift way northward. Sometimes there would be no more than a dozen, and again there would be scores. They flew in a more or less V-shaped formation, and it was an inspiring sight to see them ploughing along the blue field of heaven. Frequently two or three flocks were in sight at the same time.

About a mile down the valley, not far from the road, was a pleasant green hollow where some cows were pastured, and through the glen flowed a crystal-clear brook. The brook burst forth full-fledged from a bountiful spring, and in the pellucid depths of the pools near this spring one could get glimpses of lurking trout. Close by the stream was a cluster of pines, and one day as I was passing I noticed among the trees two men who had a little fire. I went into the grove and joined them. They spoke of themselves as "bums,' or "hoboes," but affirmed that they were not tramps. "A tramp," they explained, "never works, but a hobo is a man who travels on the road and does work when he can find a job."

They even entered on a learned disquisition as to the origin of the word hobo for they were men of intelligence and some education. They had "travelled from A to Z" in every state of the Union, and one of them said, "There's very few has more knowledge of places and routes than I have. I could pass a better civil service examination than any mail agent on this railroad that goes through here."

The night previous, they had bunked in a box car that had a little straw in it. The sun had warmed the car so it retained its heat till about midnight, but after that it became so cold the hoboes crawled out and went down the railroad and built a fire. "Yes, there are discomforts," they said, "and yet this is a very healthy life, and we never have any trouble with our stomachs or our lungs. A sick man couldn't do better than to find a good pardner, take along a little money and start out on the road."

The men seemed very leisurely. In fact, "a tramp doesn't care whether he gets to town this week or next. He knows the town will be there when he arrives."

My companions spoke of the grove they were in

as the "Hoboes' Jungle," and said that men of their sort were there nearly every day. They had several paper bags and parcels of provisions and were preparing dinner. The younger man acted as chef, and the older said, "I never was much of a jungle cook, but I can wash the dishes and get the firewood."

Dishes were plenty, such as they were. There were tin cans and pails in great variety, and there was a stew-pan, a frying-pan and a large pot and a number of low, pan-like dishes the hoboes had themselves shaped out of pieces of tin. The frequenters of this jungle never washed their pots and pans after they finished a feast, but left that job for the next men. The older of the two bums took the pot, and with a rag and some sand gave the inside a thorough scouring. Then he washed it at the stream side and plugged up a

hole with a bit of wood. He brought it full of water to his comrade who was paring potatoes. Afterward he returned to the brook with several other cans and pails which he also cleansed and put in order. One of them he filled from the stream and set on the fire to boil for the coffee. Last of all he went into the neighboring woods and gathered an armful of fallen branches, broke them up and adjusted the pieces on a rough circle of stones that served for a fireplace.

"Now," said the cook, "we want some ladles."

"All right," responded the other, "I never seen the time when I couldn't jump into the bush and make a set of kitchen tools in about fifteen minutes, if I was real hungry."

He got out his jackknife, selected some pieces of wood that suited his purpose, and soon had fashioned two rough paddles. Besides the potatoes, or "spuds" as they called them, the cook prepared two large onions and fried a good-sized piece of steak. He had some little packages of salt and pepper which he drew on for flavoring. The work was done with a good deal of deftness, but it took considerable time. However, he said that preparing the food was not nearly so much of a task as getting it in the first place.

"What'll you have for a plate?" asked the cook, turning to his pard.

"Here's a flat tin dish that'll do," replied the older man, "only I must burn it out first."

When everything was ready the cook put half the great mess of potatoes and onions into the burned-out dish, together with half the steak, while he reserved his share in the frying-pan. Then a loaf of bread was taken out of a parcel and the two sat down on some oil-cans turned bottom upward and ate in great contentment.

"This is a pretty spot," observed the older man, "and I always do like to eat where I can hear the sound of running water."

They did not pause till the last morsel was gone, and I imagine it was the only square meal they had that day. After it was done, one got out his pipe and the other his chewing tobacco. They had some thought of applying for work in the local mills. If they decided to go on to other regions they would travel by train. Often they were permitted to ride on a freight train in return for helping the train crew with their work. If permission was refused they stowed themselves away somewhere in or about the cars. Very likely they would get put off. Usually this was done at some stop the train made, and the hobo then spoke of himself as "being ditched." Occasionally the train men would push a hobo off while the train was going, and in the hobo's phraseology he then "hit the grit." At times, they sneaked a ride on a passenger coach—perhaps up on top or on the platform of the "blind baggage" coach next to the tender, or perhaps rode seated on the trucks down beneath the cars. "It ain't a bad place under there," declared the older man, "when the dust don't fly too bad, and I've seen trains carryin' more passengers on the trucks than was in the coaches."

"I told you I'd been to every state in the Union," said the younger man. "Besides that I've been to Honolulu and to Mexico. Mexico is called the land of tomorrow. It's the motto of that country never to do today what you can put off till the next day, and California is just the same. That's the effect of the climate, I suppose, and I won't dispute but what the climate is fine. However, if you want a hobo tourist's idea of California, I'd say that this state is nine-tenths climate and one-tenth business. The hobo that wants to come to a starvation country had better come here. Instead of eating three meals a day he gets only one meal in three days. They call this God's country, but I tell you the devil has the whole thing in hand.

"When I came out here as a young man affairs went well with me for a time and I got to own two good ranches. Yes, I made barrels of money. Then come a dry year and everything run behind. My stock was starving and I shot forty of my horses to put 'em out of misery. Others I sold to a rich ranchman at a dollar a head. The best of 'em he shipped to Nevada to graze, and the rest he killed and fed to his hogs. In addition to losing by the drouth, I speculated in mining stocks and kept sending good money after bad till I lost all I had.

"This state is overrated. People back East hear about the fruit and the sunshine and the flowers the year around, and the railroads advertise, and the land sharks tell how this is the finest spot on earth to really enjoy livin', and that when a person dies here he gets a ticket right from this glorious climate straight up into heaven with no change of cars. Lots of Eastern people believe this is all as represented. A family comes early in the year from the snows and frosts of their home winter. Here things are green, and the real estate agent knows the new-comers are green too. He shows 'em a place, and says, 'Now this is a nice ranch, and you can raise anything in the world on it. The price is so and so. We're almost giving it away, as it were, but we want intelligent liberal people of your class to settle here.'

"The man's wife, she looks around, and she says, 'Just see the sunshine, and the oranges, and all those roses. I guess we'd better have it.'

"So the man buys. But in a year or two there's a change in his sentiments, and the wife ain't quite satisfied. She gets to longin' for the East, and she speaks to her husband and tells him things don't seem to be just as they was represented. That's what he thinks, too, and he's ready to do whatever he can to please her, so he goes to the agent he bought of and says he wants to sell.

" 'Why, it's foolish to do that," the agent says. "Prices have dropped and at present you'd lose.'

"But the man wants to quit, and the agent makes him an offer. 'The way things are now,' he says, 'that's the best I can do.'

"The man sells and goes back East where he come from a few thousand dollars poorer than when he left. The neighbors ask how it happens he didn't stay, and he tells 'em, 'They don't have snow out there, and that's about the only unpleasant feature they lack.'

"You talk up California to any people in the East who have lived out here and they'll run you off the place. Irrigation is the only salvation for this West Coast land and, by the way, did you ever notice how the natives spit to help out the work of the streams? I chew tobacco myself, but I ain't a savage. The tobacco users in this country act as if they owned the air, and the floors of public buildings and railroad cars, not to mention the earth. They are irrigating all the time wherever they are, indoors and out, till a decent man is disgusted.

"They say it is dreadful easy to make a livin' in the fruit business, but I tell 'em I ain't seen anyone knockin' oranges out of the trees with a gold brick—

no, not a single instance of that kind. It's claimed that the San Joaquin Valley is one of the most fertile valleys in the world, and so it is in spots. But watch out for the hardpan. That is the great backfall in this country. Often the soil lies so thin on top of it that it's just about worthless. Horned toads wouldn't live on it. But the people in this country are what you call flimflammers, or, in other words, four-flushers. They lay off that hardpan desert into fruit ranches and induce people to leave their happy homes in the East to settle on it. A Californian expects you to give him all the money you've got and thank him for taking it. He sticks you with that land, and you build a shanty on it and put up a windmill and supply the wind yourself. Sheep can barely exist on the soil, and it won't raise white beans.

"Do you know about the mosquitoes? You walk along the Sacramento or the San Joaquin rivers, and the mosquitoes rise in swarms and follow you in droves, and there's terrible malaria in those valleys. Lots of ranchers have to go to the seashore in the summer to spend a couple of months, and you'd be surprised to see how wrinkly and dark and sick they look. Some owners, just in self-defense, lease their land to the Chinamen and live in the city themselves. Chinamen don't have malaria. They are very careful. They scrape their tongues at night with a piece of wood. I've watched 'em, and they bathe their feet before goin' to bed. They always boil their drinkin' water, too, and never take any in its original form, but add a little tea."

"I'll tell you another thing," said the older hobo. "I'm an ex-pugilist, but the fleas down there in Southern California have knocked me down and jumped on me. Of course, 'em real bad till summer, get don't you though there's some all the year."

"Any hobo who wants to get work on a ranch here has got to carry his own blankets," remarked the younger man. "On the farms back East the hired man has a room in the house and he sits at the family table to eat. Here they want the workingman to knuckle down and show his inferiority. Unless he's got his blankets on his back and will sleep on the straw in the barn it's not easy to find a job. 'Blanket stiffs' is what we call fellers who go about with their bedding. A stiff, you know, is a man who's dead—that is, one who's broke so often he don't really count in the world."

"A man with a farm here don't begin to get the comfort out of it he would in the East," declared the other hobo. "Fifty acres of good land there will support him handsomely, and he'll raise all his own vegetables, meat and everything. Out here he may have a much bigger place, but he'll raise just one thing—fruit, or cattle, or whatever he chooses, and buy the rest, or do without. There's people in this country with thousands of cattle who don't milk a single cow and they use condensed milk."

"One reason why we have trouble in getting work here," said the younger man, "is because employers all give preference to natives. You take it there at San Francisco, if you're a native son, they extend the glad hand and either give you a job or find one for you. There's a society they call 'Native Sons of the Golden West'—Gloomy West, it ought to be—and it would describe the members more accurately if they called them 'Native Drunks.' They're wine and steam-beer fiends, especially on the day when they gather by thousands to have their annual powwow. A native son won't do you any kind of a favor without expecting you to grease his hand a little on the side, and we all despise a California hobo. If there's a bunch of us together, and a native son comes along we won't feed him or let him come within forty rods of our camp. It's easy to get the best of 'em. They're not very sharp. You'd be surprised to see how simple some of these native sons are. Why, there was one of 'em who'd always lived in the hills, and he concluded he'd travel East. He'd never seen a railroad, and when he'd bought his ticket and the engine came snorting along the track he was so afraid of the monster he wanted to run away. They could only get him on the train by blindfolding him and backing him up on from a cattle shute."

"Well, I've got even with a few of 'em for their meanness," said the older hobo. "I've done quite a little canvassing out here, and if I'm sober I have a very good address and can make good money. One spell I put in selling nice gold watches for twenty dollars, or perhaps eighteen. They cost me three. Another while I sold harness-dressing that I manufactured myself. I'd explain how it would make the leather soft and pliable and increase the durability, and I did well. Once I had twenty-seven hundred dollars ahead, but it seemed to get away from me. I never was inclined to hoard my money, and I could never save what I earned for more than a short time.

"My best profit came from a home dressmaking pattern. It was a kind of a disk made to look like leather and there were holes punched in it. They cost me fifty cents and was marked five dollars, but I told people that the manufacturers allowed me to introduce 'em at two-fifty. They sold quick, and often people who didn't buy would have me make a pattern for which they'd pay fifty cents. I could most always get feed for my horse and lodging for myself free by making a few patterns at the ranches where I stopped.

"But it's much harder to sell to a California woman than it is to an Eastern woman. The climate seems to have a tendency to make people nervous and crazy. A woman here is always in a fidget, and at the same time she may not be doing anything, and there's no use whatever tryin' to transact business with 'em after noon. You couldn't sell a California woman a twenty-dollar gold piece for a nickel then. She either wants to take a nap, or to go out on the street to display her finery."

Two other hobo couples now arrived in the grove. They had parcels of food under their arms, and began dinner preparations. Each couple had their own fire, and did their housekeeping separately, but there was a friendly interchange of certain portions of the bill of fare. One party lacked coffee and bread. These things were supplied by the other, which in return received some bacon fat to fry eggs in and several other small items. One of my earlier acquaintances got out a piece of soap and washed his hands and face in a pail of warm water. Then he went to the stream and washed an extra shirt he carried and hung it on the bushes. Lastly, he shaved himself. In the sheltered glade loitering among the shadows of the grove with its carpet of pine needles, and lulled by the gentle warmth of the weather and by the singing stream, the hobo life had a flavor quite alluring. Certainly the hoboes themselves seemed content and even happy.

The next morning the crown of the mighty Shasta was hidden by mists, and my landlady said, "It's an old Indian sign that when there's a cloud-cap on Shasta, 'he talkee storm.' "

Sure enough, the weather was threatening all day, and we had sprinkles of rain and could see the snow-squalls whirling across the white mountain wastes. The hired girl looked from the back door up at the wild clouds hovering about the giant mountain, and said, "I told 'em yesterday it was goin' to storm, and I've come out a winner."

Though Shasta's topmost peak is 14,400 feet above the sea level, the climb to it is not especially difficult or dangerous, and many persons make the ascent every year. July and August are the best months for this, as then the weather is sure to be good and there is comparatively little snow. The climbers and their guide drive up to the timber line and camp for the night. At three the next morning they leave their horses and go the rest of the way on foot. Five hours of ascent takes them to the top, and they have ample time to look off on the world below and to descend by nightfall to the village whence they started. The entire cost for parties of ten or more is five dollars each. For a single person, the charge is twenty dollars.

The mountain with its hoary peaks and its shaggy base is always impressive, and one is reminded of the Alps, yet it lacks something of their charm, for there you have a mystery of atmosphere you seldom get in our land, and the vales about are pastoral and gentle. Then, too, there are rustic homes and quaint villages and peasant life in keeping, or in interesting contrast, with the scene. But in America the foreground is only wilderness or ruined forest, blasted by the ravages of the lumbermen, and the buildings are unsightly sawmills and temporary shacks for the help, and if there is a village it is altogether crude and unromantic.

Note:

The Shasta region is a land for the lover of the beautiful with the pioneer instinct. There is fishing and hunting and mineral springs and the most impressive of scenery. Many resorts have come into existence in the neighborhood where one can stop with entire comfort, such as Sisson, Mott, Shasta Springs and Crag View. The climb to the summit of the white peak affords an exhilarating experience, and the acquaintance one makes with the wilderness around is certain to leave many pleasant memories.

ABOUT THE AUTHOR

A prolific author, editor, photographer and illustrator, Clifton Johnson produced more than 125 books and countless articles during his long career.

His travel books, including the Highways and Byways of America series, were perhaps his most popular. A self-described folklorist, he focused almost exclusively on the rural countryside and the inhabitants of small towns and farmlands as he crisscrossed the United States, England, Scotland, Ireland and France collecting stories, taking photographs and drawing pictures.

A friend of the naturalist John Burroughs and acquaintance of many of the authors and editors of his day, Johnson lived from 1865 to 1940.

AMERICAN HIGHWAYS & BYWAYS SERIES

Highways and Byways of the Pacific Coast
Highways and Byways of the Rocky Mountains
Highways and Byways of the Mississippi Valley
Highways and Byways of the Great Lakes
Highways and Byways of the South
Highways and Byways of from the St. Lawrence
to Virginia
Highways and Byways of New England

www.ingramcontent.com/pod-product-compliance
Lightning Source LLC
Chambersburg PA
CBHW051516030726
47592CB00006B/2293